Seal of the State of Maine

CHRONOLOGY AND DOCUMENTARY
HANDBOOK OF THE
STATE OF
MAINE

974.1

ROBERT I. VEXLER

State Editor

WILLIAM F. SWINDLER

Series Editor

1978 OCEANA PUBLICATIONS, INC./Dobbs Ferry, New York

Library of Congress Cataloging in Publication Data

Main entry under title:

Chronology and documentary handbook of the State of Maine.

    (Chronologies and documentary handbooks of the States;
v. 19)
    Bibliography: p.
    Includes index.
    SUMMARY: A chronology of historical events from 1497
to 1977 with a directory of prominent citizens and copies of
pertinent documents.
    1. Maine — History — Chronology. 2. Maine —
Biography. 3. Maine — History — Sources. [1. Maine —
History] I. Vexler, Robert I. II. Series.
F19.C47   974.1   78-6942
ISBN 0-379-16144-3

Manufactured in the United States of America

TABLE OF CONTENTS

778436

ACKNOWLEDGMENT

Special recognition should be accorded Melvin Hecker, whose research has made a valuable contribution to this volume.

Thanks to my wife, Francine, in appreciation of her help in the preparation of this work.

Thanks also to my children, David and Melissa, without whose patience and understanding I would have been unable to devote the considerable time necessary for completing the state chronology series.

Robert I. Vexler

INTRODUCTION

This projected series of <u>Chronologies and Documen-</u>
<u>tary Handbooks of the States</u> will ultimately comprise
fifty separate volumes - one for each of the states of
the Union. Each volume is intended to provide a concise
ready reference of basic data on the state, and to serve
as a starting point for more extended study as the individual user may require. Hopefully, it will be a
guidebook for a better informed citizenry - students,
civic and service organizations, professional and business personnel, and others.

The editorial plan for the <u>Handbook</u> series falls
into six divisions: (1) a chronology of selected events
in the history of the state; (2) a short biographical
directory of the principal public officials, e.g.,
governors, Senators and Representatives; (3) a short
biographical directory of prominent personalities of
the state (for most states); (4) the first state constitution; (5) the text of some representative documents
illustrating main currents in the political, economic,
social or cultural history of the state: and (6) a
selected bibliography for those seeking further or more
detailed information. Most of the data found in the
present volume, in fact, have been taken from one or
another of these references.

The current constitutions of all fifty states, as
well as the federal Constitution, are regularly kept up
to date in the definitive collection maintained by the
Legislative Drafting Research Fund of Columbia University and published by the publisher of the present series of <u>Handbooks</u>. These texts are available in most
major libraries under the title, <u>Constitutions of the</u>
<u>United States: National and State</u>, in two volumes, with
a companion volume, the <u>Index Digest of State Constitu-</u>
<u>tions</u>.

Finally, the complete collection of documents il-
lustrative of the constitutional development of each
state, from colonial or territorial status up to the
current constitution as found in the Columbia University
collection, is being prepared for publication in a mul-
ti-volume series by the present series editor. Whereas
the present series of <u>Handbooks</u> is intended for a wide
range of interested citizens, the series of annotated
constitutional materials in the volumes of <u>Sources and</u>
<u>Documents of U. S. Constitutions</u> is primarily for the
specialist in government, history or law. This is not
to suggest that the general citizenry may not profit
equally from referring to these materials; rather, it
points up the separate purpose of the <u>Handbooks</u>, which

is to guide the user to these and other sources of au-
thoritative information with which he may systematically
enrich his knowledge of this state and its place in the
American Union.

William F. Swindler
Series Editor

Robert I. Vexler
Series Associate Editor

I Guide

State Motto

CHRONOLOGY

1497   John Cabot was sent out by Henry VII to America. He traveled along the coast of Maine and thus established the first claim to Maine for England.

1524   Giovanni da Verrazano, in the employ of the French, traveled along the Maine coast and sailed among the islands, establishing a tenuous claim for France.

1525   Estéban Gomez explored Maine's coast.

1556   André Thevet of France, a scholar and noted writer, visited Maine with an exploring party.

1597   Simon Ferdinando, a Portugese navigator, working for England traveled along the coast of Maine.

1602   Bartholomew Gosnold arrived in Maine on board his ship, the Concord. He returned to England with furs, cedar and sassafras from southern Maine.

1603   April. Martin Pring sighted the region of Penobscot Bay on his voyage to America. He then explored the coast of Maine.

Henry IV, King of France granted De Monts the territory between 40 and 46 degrees North with the name of Acadie or Acadia.

1604   Pierre du Gast, the Sieur de Monts brought a group of men to America, landing with them on Dochet Island in the St. Croix River. It was off the area which is now called Calais, Maine. They remained on the island for the winter, but decided that it was not a good site for a colony. The navigator Samuel de Champlain sailed south along the coast and finally selected Port Royal on the Bay of Fundy.

1605   May 17. Captain George Weymouth landed on Monhegan Island which he named St. George. His men, from the ship, Archangel, traded with the Indians. The expedition had been fitted out by Sir Ferdinando Gorges, the Earl of Southampton and the Earl of Arundel. The expedition also explored the coast of Maine.

October. Sir John Popham, a member of the
Plymouth Company, which had been granted
land from the 41st to the 45th North Lati-
tude, sponsored an expedition under Captain
Martyn Pryn. The captain was to explore the
coast of Maine and settle a group of colonists
there. James I had granted the charter to
the company.

Sir Ferdinando Gorges and his associates
hired Henry Challons to take a group of
colonists on board the <u>Richard of Plymouth</u>
to Maine. Challons was not very effective.
The ship arrived near Puerto Rico where it
was seized by the Spaniards, and everyone was
taken prisoner.

1607   May 31. A colony of 120 under George Popham
and Raleigh Gilbert, sponsored by the Plymouth Company, left Plymouth.

August 6. George Popham and his group of
colonists approached land at the mouth
of the Kennebec River with caution.

August 7. The colonists landed on the coast
north of Monhegan Island. They then sailed
to Popham Beach.

August 14. The colonists sailed up the Saga-
hadoc River.

August 19. The Plymouth Company colonists
landed on the peninsula of Sabino. They
began to construct a fort and storehouse on
August 20. Many of the colonists left in
December, and the remainder adandoned the
colony in the spring of 1608.

1608   Winter. The ship, the <u>Virginia</u>, which had
been constructed by the colonists sailed
for England with a cargo of Maine furs and
sassafras root. Travel continued between England and Virginia for twenty years.

1609   Henry Hudson, an Englishman in the employ of
the Dutch, explored the Maine coast. He
landed and made some repairs on his ship with
Maine pine. This was the first such recorded
repair.

French Jesuits Biard and Masse founded a
fortified mission on the island of Mount

Desert.

1610   Driven off course on his way from Virginia
            to England, Samuel Argalls arrived on the
            Maine coast and landed, remaining there for
            a short period of time.

            Jean de Biencourt settled at Port Royal with
            the two Jesuit priests, Father Biard and
            Father Massé.

1613   Samuel Argalls led a group of French settlers,
            who had been forced out by the English at
            Jamestown, to establish a small French set-
            tlement at Somes Sound near Mount Desert on
            the coast of Maine.

1614   John Smith explored and mapped the coast of
            Maine and New England. He gave the country
            the name of New England.

1615   Sir Richard Hawkins picked up a cargo of fur
            pelts along the Maine coast and sold them in
            Europe at a handsome profit.

1616   Sir Ferdinando Gorges invested all his pos-
            sessions in a small ship under the command
            of Captain Richard Vines and a group of 16
            men. They founded a colony on the Sasco
            River near what is now Biddeford Pool. They
            sent good reports back to England.

1618   Sir Ferdinando Gorges was able to persuade
            the Plymouth Company to send two men to spend
            the winter at Monhegan and make a settlement.

1620   November 30. Following the surrender by the
            Plymouth Company of its charter, King James I
            granted the "Great Patent of New England."
            The limits were established from 40 degrees
            North Latitude to 48 degrees North Latitude
            and from sea to sea.

1622   August 10. The Council of New England granted
            all the land between the Merrimac and Kennebec
            Rivers, present-day Maine and New Hampshire,
            to Sir Ferdinando Gorges and John Mason. The
            name Province of Maine was used for the first
            time in this grant. The two men divided the
            territory: Gorges took the portion between
            Piscataqua and the Kennebec in 1629, and Mason
            the remainder.

1623   Kittery was founded. It was the first town
            to be incorporated in 1647.

            The first permanent settlement was made in
            what is now Biddeford.

            Christopher Leavitt, the first settler in
            the Casco Bay region spent his first winter
            on House Island.

1625   July 12. The Indians Pemaquid, Samoset, and
            Unongoit purportedly sold a large amount of
            land to John Brown, a fur trader who came to
            the area to live. The region comprised the
            present towns of Bristol and Damariscotta.

1627   Abraham Jennings and Company sold Monhegan
            Island and their stock in trade.

1628   The Plymouth Pilgrims chose several sites for
            fur trading posts. Machias did not last very
            long because it was captured by the French.
            Pentaguet on Penobscot Bay later became Cas-
            tine and continued for seven years until
            the French also put this post out of business.
            Cushnoc, which later became August, the state
            capital, located 40 miles up the Kennebec
            River lasted for about forty years.

            Thomas Purchase established his settlement
            at Pejepscot, now Brunswick.

1629   The region was divided between Sir Ferdinando
            Gorges and John Mason. Gorges retained the
            area of the present state of Maine.

            January 13. The Pilgrims applied to the
            New England Company and obtained a grant of
            land on the Kennebec River.

            Aldworth and Eldridge received a grant for the
            town of Bristol.

1630   Two grants of land were made. Thomas Lewis
            and Richard Bonuthon received land on the
            north side of the Saco River at Winter Harbor
            or Biddeford Pool. John Oldham and Richard
            Vines received the land on the other side
            of the river.

            June 26. Lygonia or Plough Patent was grant-
            ed.

The land west of the river was granted to Beauchamp and Leverett, the Muscargus or Waldo Patent.

1631   February 29. The Council of New England granted the Pemaquid patent to Aldworth and Eldridge.

November 4. Richard Bradshaw received the Pejepscot Grant. This consisted of 1,500 acres of land at the head of the Pejepscot River on the north side.

December 1. Robert Trelawney and Moses Goodyer received the Cape Elizabeth Grant, consisting of 1,500 acres of land between the grant made to Cammock and the bay and the Casco River.

December 2. John Stratton received the Cape Porpoise Grant, which consisted of 2,000 acres. Thomas Gorges took over this grant when he came to govern as deputy for Sir Ferdinando Gorges in 1640.

December 2. The New England Council granted to Ferdinando Gorges, grandson of Sir Ferdinando, Walter Norton and others 1,200 acres of land on each side of the Agamenticus (York) River.

1632   June. A group of French buccaneers, led by D'Aulney, raided the Pilgrim trading post at Castine.

1633   M. La Tour captured the Machias trading post.

1634   John Mason introduced the first sawmill in York.

1635   February. The Council of New England returned its charter.

1637   July 23. King Charles I made Sir Ferdinando Gorges governor of all New England.

1639   April 13. King Charles I confirmed Gorges' patent. He also changed the name of the province from New Somersetshire to the Province of Maine.

1640   Thomas Gorges came to Maine as deputy governor to govern for Sir Ferdinando Gorges.

1642   George Cleeve went to England where he per-
            suaded Sir Alexander Rigby to purchase the
            old Lygonia patent. Cleeve had already
            obtained his patent at Casco which had been
            given to him by Gorges in 1637.

1649   October 16. The independent government of
            Maine passed an act which granted the right
            to form churches to all Christians providing
            that they led moral lives.

            Father Gabriel Druillettee left Quebec with
            Indian guides. They landed on the Kennebec
            River at Norridgewock where Druillettee
            founded a mission to convert the Indians to
            Catholicism in order to counteract the Eng-
            lish Protestant influence.

1652   May 31. Disregarding an appeal to Parliament,
            the Massachusetts General Court ruled that
            Maine was a part of the Massachusetts Bay
            Colony. Maine was unable to resist and was
            annexed.

            July. Massachusetts commissioners appeared
            at Kittery where they held a conference to
            set up a government for the region. Governor
            Godfrey protested that he would not accept
            the authority of Massachusetts.

            July 4. Ligonia was annexed by the colony
            of Massachusetts.

            November 20. Kittery was annexed by Massachu-
            setts Bay Colony.

            November 20. York County was established,
            with its seat at Alfred. It was named for
            James, Duke of York, who later became James
            II.

            November 22. York was annexed by Massachu-
            setts.

1653   Wells, Cape Elizabeth, and Saco submitted to
            the rule of Massachusetts.

1658   Scarborough and Falmouth agreed to accept
            the control of Massachusetts.

1665   The mast trade with England was doing quite
            well.

1668   July 6. A special convention was held at
              York which recognized the authority of Massa-
              chusetts.

1675   The Indians attacked the settlements of
              Casco, Pemaquid, Cape Neddick, Black Point,
              and Arrowsic which were burned. The Indians
              either killed or abducted the population
              during King Philip's War.

1677   March 13. John Usher, agent of the Massachu-
              setts authorities, purchased the Gorges
              claim from his heirs for Ł1,250 (approximate-
              ly $6,000). Massachusetts thus gained a clear
              title to Maine.

1688   Edward Randolph made the first survey of
              Maine.

1689   April. Sir Thomas Danforth took charge of
              the government.

              June. Dover was attacked and destroyed by
              the Indians. Twenty-nine captives were
              taken and sold to the French.

              August 2. Moxus of the Penobscot Indian
              tribe attacked and destroyed Pemaquid.

              August. Major Swain drove the Indians away
              from Scarborough and Falmouth.

1690   March. M. D'Artel led the French troops, and
              Hopehood led the Indians in an attack upon
              Newichawannock, later Berwick. The settle-
              ment was completely destroyed.

              May. Approximately 400 to 500 Frenchmen and
              Indians arrived at Casco Bay. They destroyed
              the settlement of Casco and then attacked Fort
              Loyal.

              May. Sir William Phipps took Fort Royal.

1691   June. Approximately 200 Indians led by Moxus
              attacked the fort at Wells. Moxus and his
              Indians were repelled and then went to Cape
              Neddock in York.

1692   Spring. King William IV gave Massachusetts
              a new charter which included all of Acadia
              and Maine.

1700   March. The British Parliament passed a law
         ordering that the Catholic missionaries, who
         were accused of trying to convince the Indi-
         ans to renounce their allegiance to the Bri-
         tish crown, to leave Maine before September
         10.

1702   June 11. Joseph Dudley, who had been ap-
         pointed governor of the New England provin-
         ces by Queen Anne, arrived in New England.

1703   June 20. Governor Joseph Dudley arranged
         a meeting with the Indians at Falmouth.
         Sagamores and members of the Pennacooks,
         Sokokis, Anasagunticooks, Canabas, and Tar-
         ratines were present. They signed a treaty
         several days later.

         August. Approximately 500 Frenchmen and In-
         dians crossed the eastern frontier of Maine.
         They attacked several settlements, destroying
         Wells, Cape Porpoise and Winter Harbor, as
         well as Spurwink and Purpooduck.

1713   Berwick was incorporated.

1715   The government of Massachusetts ordered a
         road constructed between Berwick and Pejes-
         cot.

1722   June. Some homes at Merry Meeting Bay were
         destroyed.

         **September. Approximately 400-500 Indians
         attacked Arrowsic.**

1725   December 15. Four chiefs came to sign a
         treaty of peace in Boston.

1726   July 30. Governor Drummer met with the
         Indians to discuss the articles of the peace
         treaty of December 1725. Wenemovet and twen-
         ty-five Sagamores signed the treaty.

1742   Population: 12,000.

1745   The Indians attacked St. George's Fort on
         the St. George River. The settlers and
         troops defeated the Indians.

         June. Sir William Pepperell took Louis-
         bourg.

1746   The Indians attacked the towns of Gorham, Pemaquid, Wiscasset and Falmouth.

1749   The Indians attacked the towns of Scarborough, Sacarappa, Falmouth, Pemaquid, and Damariscotta.

1753   June. Several businessmen and professional men in Boston formed an association to purchase the land formerly held in Maine by the Colony of New Plymouth. They called themselves the Proprietors of the Kennebec Purchase, or the Fifty Associates.

1758   Frenchmen and Indians were driven back from Fort St. George and Meduncook, later Friendship.

1759   Fort Pownal was planned and constructed.

1760   Estimated population: 20,000.

            May 28. Cumberland and Lincoln Counties were established. Cumberland, with its county seat at Portland, was named for William Augustus, Duke of Cumberland, second son of George II and Queen Caroline. Lincoln, with its seat at Wiscasset, was named for Benjamin Lincoln.

1762   The General Court of Massachusetts responded to a petition of the residents of Maine and organized twelve townships between Penobscot and the St. Croix Rivers.

1770   Estimated population: 31,257.

1773   Thomas McIntyre constructed the first lime kiln at Thomaston.

1775   March. Captain Henry Mowatt seized the guns and ammunition of Fort Pownal for Britain.

            May 12. The first naval action of the Revolutionary War occurred when the patriots were able to capture the British sloop _Margaretta_ off Machias, Maine.

            September 9. Benedict Arnold sailed from Newburyport with his troops for Canada. They followed the Kennebec and Dead Rivers on the expedition to Quebec.

October 18. Captain Henry Mowatt bombarded
Falmouth. All the public buildings, as well
as many homes and warehouses were destroyed.

A Committee of Safety and Inspection was
elected at Falmouth. Notice was given that
English goods were not to be unloaded at
Falmouth.

The town of Machias had a well-developed lumber business.

1777   August. The British sent a small fleet to
        attempt to take the small sea coast town of
        Machias which had been made a military sta-
        tion by the colonists and was supplied with
        two nine-pounders and garrisoned by 300 men.
        The British failed to take the town.

1778   The Continental Congress divided Massachu-
        setts into three admiralty districts, one of
        which was the District of Maine.

1779   June. General Francis McLane left Halifax
        with eight ships and 900 men. They were to
        capture Castine in the Penobscot Bay area
        and were successful. The British began to
        construct fortifications. Mowatt remained
        in the vicinity to help with three sloops.

        July 28. American troops commanded by Briga-
        dier Genetal Solomon Lovell and General Peleg
        Wadsworth appeared at Castine. The Americans
        lost 100 men, and the British only 30. The
        American forces might have been able to take
        the town if Commodore Dudley Saltonstall of
        New Haven, Connecticut had been willing to
        bring his ships into action. Two weeks later
        British reinforcements arrived, and the Ameri-
        cans had to retreat. Saltonstall was not
        able to stop the British fleet. As a result
        the British held the entire eastern coast of
        Maine.

        The Continental Congress put an embargo on all
        goods or food exported from the District of
        Maine in order to prevent these goods from
        falling into British hands.

1780   Estimated population: 49,133.

1781   General Peleg Wadsworth, who had been placed
        in command of the District of Maine, was cap-

tured by the British. He was taken to Fort
George at Castine and imprisoned, having
been wounded in the arm. His wife and friend
were allowed to visit him. Major Burton, who
was captured a little later, and Wadsworth
escaped when they learned that they would
soon be taken to England.

1784   A land office was established.

1785   January 1. Maine's first newspaper, The
            Falmouth Gazette, appeared at Falmouth, now
            Portland.

            January. A convention was held at Falmouth
            to discuss various grievances against Eng-
            land.

1786   January 4. Another convention was held at
            Falmouth where grievances were drafted and
            presented to the government officials.

            March. Drawings for the Massachusetts Lot-
            tery were held. The money paid in was to help
            the state pay for the debts contraced during
            the Revolutionary War. The land offered
            consisted of fifty townships each six miles
            square totalling 1,107,396 acres located be-
            tween the Penobscot and the St. Croix Rivers.
            2,720 tickets were sold at ₤60 per ticket.
            Every ticket would grant the holder a prize,
            the smallest being half a mile square, the
            highest a township.

1787   January. A convention met with a vote being
            taken for separation from Massachusetts.
            645 favored separation, and 349 were against.
            No action was taken, however.

            A stagecoach line was opened between Portland
            and Portsmouth. In 1806 it was extended
            to Augusta.

1789   June 25. Hancock and Washington Counties
            were established. Hancock, with its seat at
            Ellsworth, was named for John Hancock, the
            first signer of the Declaration of Indepen-
            dence and the first governor of the Common-
            wealth of Massachusetts. Washington, effec-
            tive May 1, 1790, with its seat at Machias,
            was named for George Washington, commander
            of the Continental Army and first President

of the United States.

1790   Population 96,540.

The government divided Maine into nine commercial districts and appointed a collector
and other custom house officials for each
area.

Portland Head Lighthouse was established.

1794   June 24. The Massachusetts legislature chartered Maine's first college, Bowdoin College,
at Brunswick. It was named for Governor
James Bowdoin. The first class entered in
1802. The state granted the college five
townships for its support.

The Jay Treaty was signed. Article 5 provided
for a commission which was to decide which
body of water was actually the St. Croix
River. This commission in 1798 defined
the St. Croix as follows: the mouth of the
river is in the Passamaquoddy bay. In addition Mouse, Dudley and Frederick Islands were
given to the United States.

As a result of the census, Maine received
three representatives to Congress.

1795   Another convention met to discuss the issue
of separation from Massachusetts. It was
suggested that the counties of York, Cumber-
land, and Lincoln form a separate state.
Washington and Hancock Counties were to be
left under the control of Massachusetts.

1796   After having concluded his service as Secretary of War in President George Washington's
Administration, General Henry Knox retired
to Maine. He had had a mansion constructed
on the site of old Fort St. George in 1793.

1797   Another vote was taken for the separation of
Maine from Massachusetts. At this time the
people of Maine were not ready to accept
separation.

1799   February 20. Kennebec County was established,
effective April 1, 1799, with Augusta as the
county seat.

1800   Population: 151,719.

1801   Maine's first public library was established
        at Castine.

1802   The first group of students entered Bowdoin
        College at Brunswick.

1805   March 4. Oxford County was created, with
        South Paris as its county seat. It was
        named for Oxford University in England.

1807   The Massachusetts legislature passed an act
        to stop disputes over land claims.

        Twenty towns voted in favor of separation
        from Massachusetts, and thirty-five voted
        against.

1809   March 1. Somerset County, with its seat at
        Skowhegan, was created. It was named for
        Somerset County, England.

        September. Four men who were surveying land
        in the town of Malta, later Windsor, were
        attacked by a group of nine men, who were
        armed and disguised as Indians. Paul Chad-
        wick, one of the surveyors, was mortally
        wounded. The other three escaped. The men
        involved in the attack eventually surrendered.
        Their friends helped them to escape from pri-
        son during the night of October 3-4.

        November 16. The trial of the men who had
        attacked the surveyors opened. Seven men were
        indicted for the murder. Two of them only
        carried staves and were not accused. The
        jury was not able to determine who had
        actually fired the gun that killed Chadwick,
        and after two days they brought in a verdict
        of not guilty.

        The first cotton and woolen mills in North
        America were constructed at Brunswick.

1810   Population: 228,705.

1813   September 5. Captain William Burrows, com-
        manding the United States brig Enterprise,
        attacked and captured the British ship Boxer
        off the coast of Maine. He brought the ship
        into Portland on September 6. Captain Bur-
        rows was mortally wounded and died eight hours
        later.

The following academic institutions were
founded and chartered: Colby College and
the University of Maine, both at Waterville.

1814   June 20. The <u>Bulwark</u> entered the Sheepscot
and landed six barges full of marines. They
were soon driven back to their ship by the
militia.

July. The British fleet sailed across Passamaquoddy Bay and anchored off Fort Sullivan
at Eastport. Major Putnam listened to the
wishes of the people and arranged to surrender
the fort provided that the British would pa-
rade his officers. Everything was agreed to.

September 1. The British fleet arrived at
Castine and captured the town.

September. The British captured Belfast and
Frankfort.

December 28. A convention of delegates from
the Oxford County towns met and indicated
their dissatisfaction because of the lack of
support offered the people of Maine by the
Massachusetts government.

1815   February 6. Petitions for separation were
sent to the Massachusetts General Court. The
legislature referred them to a committee and
tabled them. 63 towns indicated their desire
for separation, and twenty towns were opposed.

The first total abstinence society in the
world was founded in Portland.

1816   January. Many petitions were sent to the
Massachusetts General Court requesting the
separation of Maine from the state. The
legislature passed a bill which provided for
a vote on May 20.

February 15. Penobscot County was created,
effective April 1, 1816, with Bangor as its
county seat.

May 20. The residents of Maine voted on the
proposition for separation from Massachusetts.
10,584 voted in favor and 6,491 indicated
their opposition. Less than fifty per cent
of the voters cast their ballots. The results
of the election were given to the committee

of the General Court for further study.

September 2. Another vote was held on the
issue of separation from Massachusetts.
11,969 voted in favor and 10,347 against.
However, the Massachusetts legislature required that a majority of five to four had
to favor separation. It established a complicated vote counting process whereby it
showed that the ayes had gained victory by
a slight majority.

September 30. A convention met at Brunswick
to consider separation. They decided that
the complicated counting system indicated a
majority in favor of separation.

December 3. The General Court received the
report of its committee in regard to the issue of Maine's separation. The legislature
later decided that the people of Maine did
not want separation.

1817   A small group of Americans penetrated the
          wilderness up the St. John River and formed
          the small settlement of Madawaska.

1819   April 19. A committee of the Maine members
          of the Massachusetts legislature issued an
          address to the people of the District of Maine
          urging them to vote for those representatives
          who supported separation.

          May 31. The state legislature received 94
          petitions favoring separation by this date.

          July 26. Another general vote was held on
          the issue of separation. 17,091 voted in
          favor and 7,132 against. A 1,500 majority
          was required in favor of separation.

          September 21. Delegates were elected for
          a constitutional convention to meet in Port-
          land on the second Monday in October.

          October 11. The Constitutional Convention met
          in Portland. William King was elected perma-
          nent president. King later became acting
          governor and then the first elected governor
          of the state. The state constitution was
          adopted 9,050 to 796.

1820   Population: 298,335.

February 17. Senator Thomas' compromise
amendment to the bil for the admittance of
Maine and Missouri to statehood, known as
the Missouri Compromise, was adopted.

March 3. President James Monroe signed the
Maine Bill as part of the Missouri Compromise.
Maine was to be admitted as a free state, and
Missouri was to be permitted to write its con-
stitution without any restriction in regard
to slavery.

March 15. Maine was admitted to the Union as
the 23rd state.

April. State officers were elected. William
King was elected and served until 1821.

June 9. The state seal was presented and
accepted by the state legislature. It was re-
designed in 1919.

June 19. The first state legislature of Maine
authorized Colby College to confer degrees.
It had already been chartered as the Maine
Literary and Theological Institute on February 27, 1813 by the General Court of Massachusetts, Colby awarded its first degrees in
1822.

October 30. A joint commission made up of
delegates from Massachusetts and Maine began working out the details of the separation
of the two states. They continued their work
until November 27, 1827.

1821   William Durkee Williamson, Democrat, became
            acting governor of the state and served for
            a few months.

            Benjamin Ames, Democrat, became acting gover-
            nor of Maine and served for a few months.

1822   Benjamin Ames, Democrat-Republican, became
            acting governor of the state and served for
            several months.

            Albion Keith Parris, Democrat-Republican, be-
            came governor of the state. He served in of-
            fice until 1827.

1827   February 7. Waldo County was established,
            effective July 3, 1827, with Belfast as its

county seat. It was named for Samuel Waldo,
the proprietor of Waldo patent, who had
brought 40 families to Maine from Brunswick
and Saxony in 1740.

Enoch Lincoln, Democrat-Republican, became
governor of Maine. He served in office until his death on October 8, 1829.

1829   October 8. Nathan Cutler, Democrat, became
            acting governor of Maine. He served in the
            office until 1830.

            King William of the Netherlands was selected
            as the arbitrator in the Maine dispute with
            Canada under the convention between Great
            Britain and the United States of 1827.

1830   Population: 399,455.

            Jonathan G. Hunton, Democrat, became governor
            of the state. He served until 1831.

1831   December 29. A patent was awarded to Hiram
            Avery and John Avery Pitts of Winthrop, Maine,
            for their invention of a combined portable
            thresher and fanning mill.

            King William of the Netherlands rendered his
            decision in regard to the Maine-Canada border
            dispute. Maine protested against it. The
            United States Senate did not agree to the
            decision.

            Samuel Emerson Smith, Jackson Democrat, be-
            came governor of the state. He served in
            office until 1834.

1834   Robert Pinckney Dunlop, Democrat, became
            governor of Maine. He served in the guberna-
            torial office until 1838.

1838   March 20. Franklin County was created, ef-
            fective May 9, 1838, with its seat at Farming-
            ton. It was named for Benjamin Franklin,
            American official, member of the Continental
            Congress, signer of the Declaration of Inde-
            pendence and member of the Constitutional
            Convention.

            March 23. Piscataquis County was established,
            effective April 30, 1838, with its seat at
            Dover-Foxcroft.

Edward Kent, Whig, became governor of Maine and served until 1839.

As a result of tension involved in the disputed territory between New Brunswick and Maine, the "Aroostook War" broke out and continued until 1839.

1839   January. The Maine legislature tried to prevent the British from carrying out lumbering in the Aroostock territory which was claimed by both New Brunswick and Maine.

March 16. Aroostook County was created, effective May 1, 1839, with its county seat at Houlton.

March 21. General Winfield Scott who was in command of troops at the Maine frontier arranged a truce and for joint occupancy of the territory in dispute until a satisfactory settlement should be reached by the United States and Great Britain.

John Fairfield, Democrat, became governor of Maine. He served in the office until 1841.

1840   Population: 501,793.

1841   Edward Kent, Whig, became governor of the state, in which post he served until 1842.

1842   August 9. The Webster-Ashburton Treaty was signed. The compromise settlement awarded Maine 5,500 square miles less than she claimed and gave Great Britain much less than she demanded.

John Fairfield, Democrat, became governor of Maine. He served until his resignation in 1843.

1843   Edward Kavanagh, Democrat, became acting governor of the state upon the resignation of Governor John Fairfield. Kavanagh served until 1844.

1844   Hugh J. Anderson, Democrat, became governor of Maine. He served in office until 1847.

1846   October 17. Nathan Clifford became Attorney General in the Cabinet of President James K. Polk.

The state legislature passed a prohibition law.

1847   John Winchester Dana, Democrat, became governor of the state. He served until 1850.

1849   Sarah Orre Jewett, noted authoress, was born in Maine.

1850   Population: 583,169.

John Hubbard, Democrat, became governor of the state. He served in the office until 1853.

1851   June 2. Maine passed another prohibition law which forbade the manufacture and sale of alcoholic beverages of all kinds throughout the state.

1853   William George Crosby, Whig and Free Soiler, became governor of the state. He served in office until 1855.

1854   March 18. Androscoggin County was established, effective March 31, 1854, with its seat at Auburn. It was named for the Androscoggin Indian tribe.

April 4. Sagadhoc County was created, with its county seat at Bath.

1855   Anson Peaslee Morrill, Republican, became governor of the state. He served in office until 1856.

Bates College was founded and chartered at Lewiston.

1856   Samuel Wells, Democrat, became governor of the state. He served until January 8, 1857.

1857   January 8. Hannibal Hamlin, who had been elected in 1856, a Republican, became governor of the state. He served until his resignation on February 20, 1857.

February 20. Joseph H. Williams, Republican, became acting governor of the state. He served in the office until 1858.

1858   Maine adopted prohibition again.

Lot Myrick Morrill, Republican, became governor of Maine. He served in office until 1861.

1860   Population: 628,279.

1861   Horatio King, who had been Postmaster General ad interim since January 1, 1861, became Postmaster General in the Cabinet of President James Buchanan.

November. Hannibal Hamlin was elected Vice President of the United States on the Republican ticket with Abraham Lincoln, who was elected President.

Israel Washburn, Republican, became governor of Maine. He served in office until 1863.

1863   Abner Coburn, Republican, became governor of the state. He served in the gubernatorial office until 1864.

1864   July 1. William P. Fessenden was appointed Secretary of the Treasury by President Abraham Lincoln. He assumed his office as a member of the cabinet on July 5.

Samuel Cony, Unionist Republican, became governor of the state. He served in office until 1867.

1865   February 7. The state legislature ratified the 13th Amendment to the United States Constitution.

1866   July 4. 1,500 buildings were destroyed as a result of a fire in Portland.

1867   January 19. The state legislature ratified the 14th Amendment to the United States Constitution.

Joshua Lawrence Chamberlain, Republican, became governor of the state. He served in the gubernatorial office until 1871.

1868   Pulp was first manufactured commercially at Topsham.

1869   March 11. The state legislature ratified the 15th Amendment to the United States Constitution.

1870   Population: 626,915.

                March. The state legislature passed a bill
                to encourage Swedish immigration to Maine.
                Free land and state aid was offered to those
                who were willing to come. Later on during
                the year a group of Swedish settlers arrived
                and founded the town of New Sweden.

1871   Sidney Perham, Republican, became governor
                of Maine. He served in the gubernatorial
                office until 1874.

1874   Nelson Dingley, Jr., Republican, became gov-
                ernor of the state. He served in office un-
                til 1876.

1876   June 21. Lot Myrick Morrill was appointed
                Secretary of the Treasury by President Ulysses
                S. Grant. He assumed his office as a member
                of the cabinet on July 7, 1876.

                Selden Connor, Republican, became governor
                of Maine. He served in office until 1879.

1879   Alonzo Garcelon, Democrat, became governor
                of the state and served in office until 1880.

1880   Population: 648,936.

                Daniel F. Davis, Republican, became governor
                of Maine. He served in the office until
                1881.

1881   Harris Merrill Plaisted, Democrat-Greenback,
                became governor of Maine. He served in of-
                fice until 1883.

1883   Frederick Robie, Republican, became governor
                of the state and served until 1887.

1887   Maine abolished the death penalty.

                Joseph R. Bodwell, Republican, became gover-
                nor of Maine. He served in office until his
                death on December 15, 1887.

                December 15. Sebastian S. Marble, Republi-
                can, became acting governor of the state
                upon the death of Governor Bodwell. Marble
                served in the office until 1889.

1889   March 5. James G. Blaine was appointed Secretary of State by President Benjamin Harrison. Blaine assumed his office as a member of the cabinet on March 7.

Edwin C. Burleigh, Republican, became governor of Maine. He served in the gubernatorial office until 1893.

1890   Population: 661,086.

1893   Henry B. Cleaves, Republican, became governor of the state. He served in office until January 1897.

1897   January 6. Llewellyn Powers, Republican, became governor of Maine. He served in office until January 2, 1901,

1900   Population: 694,466.

1901   January 2. John Fremont Hill, Republican, became governor of Maine. He served in the gubernatorial office until the end of his term on January 4, 1905.

1905   January 4. William T. Cobb, Republican, became governor of the state, serving until the end of his term on January 6, 1909.

Bangor Theological Seminary was founded and chartered at Bangor.

1907   The state legislature adopted an initiative and referendum law.

1909   January 6. Bert M. Fernald, Republican, became governor of the state and served until the end of his term on January 4, 1911.

1910   Population: 742,371.

1911   January 4. Frederick W. Plaisted, Democrat, became governor of the state. He served until the end of his term of office on January 1, 1913.

March 31. The state legislature ratified the 16th Amendment to the United States Constitution.

The state legislature passed a direct-primary voting law.

1912   Nasson College was founded and chartered at Springvale.

1913   January 1. William T. Haines, Republican, who had been elected in 1912, became governor of Maine. He served in the office until the end of his term on January 6, 1915.

February 20. The state legislature ratified the 17th Amendment to the United States Constitution.

1914   Maine led the nation in the production of pulp.

1915   January 6. Oakley C. Curtis, Democrat, who had been elected in 1914, became governor of the state. He served in the gubernatorial office until the end of his term on January 3, 1917.

St. Joseph's College was founded and chartered in North Windham.

1916   Acadia National Park was established. It consists of 37,005 acres.

1917   January 3. Carl E. Milliken, Republican, who had been elected in 1916, became governor. He served until January 5, 1921.

1919   January 8. The state legislature ratified the 18th Amendment to the United States Constitution.

November 5. The state legislature ratified the 19th Amendment to the United States Constitution.

George Buckrum Dorr and Dr. Charles Eliot of Harvard gave approximately 15,000 acres of land surrounding Cadillac Mountain, approximately one-fifth of Mount Desert Island, to the United States government. They were concerned with the extensive aspects of the lumbering operations on the island. Congress accepted the land, naming it Lafayette National Park. Its name was changed to Acadia National Park in 1928. Additional land was eventually donated to the government,

1920   Population: 768,014.

1921   January 5. Frederick H. Parkhurst, Republi-
            can, who had been elected in 1920, became
            governor of the state. He served in the
            office until his death at the end of the
            month, January 31.

            January 31. Percival P. Baxter, Republican,
            President of the Senate became governor of
            Maine upon the death of Frederick H. Park-
            hurst. Baxter was subsequently elected to
            the office and served until the end of his
            term on January 8, 1925.

1924   The first radio station in Maine, at Bangor,
            WABI, began broadcasting.

1925   January 8. Ralph O. Brewster, Republican,
            who had been elected in 1924, became gover-
            nor of the state. He was reelected in 1926
            and served until the end of his second term
            on January 2, 1929.

1929   January 2. William T. Gardiner, Republican,
            became governor of the state. He had been
            elected in 1928 and served until January 4,
            1933.

            The Jackson Memorial Library was established.

1930   Population: 797,423.

1932   April 1. The state legislature ratified the
            20th Amendment to the United States Consti-
            tution.

1933   January 4. Louis J. Brann, Democrat, who
            had been elected in 1932, became governor
            of the state, He served in the gubernatorial
            office until January 6, 1937.

            December 6. The state legislature ratified
            the 21st Amendment to the United States Con-
            stitution.

1937   January 6. Lewis O. Barrows, Republican,
            who had been elected in 1936, became governor
            of the state. He served in office until
            January 1, 1941.

1940   Population: 847,226.

            June 3. Margaret Chase Smith was elected to
            fill the seat left vacant by her late husband,

Clyde Harold Smith, for the remainder of
his term in the House of Representatives for
the 76th Congress. She served in the House
of Representatives for eight years and was
elected to the United States Senate in 1948.

1941   January 1. Sumner Sewall, Republican, who
            had been elected in 1940, became governor
            of the state and served until January 3, 1945.

            The Marine Maritime Academy was established
            at Castine.

1945   January 3. Horace A. Hildreth, Republican,
            who had been elected in 1944, became governor
            of Maine. He served in the office until Jan-
            uary 5, 1949.

1947   March 31. The state legislature ratified
            the 22nd Amendment to the United States Con-
            stitution.

            Most of the buildings in the Bar Harbor area
            were lost when Mount Desert Island went up in
            flames.

1948   Margaret Chase Smith became the first woman
            elected by the state to the United States
            Senate.

1949   January 5. Frederick G. Payne, Republican,
            who had been elected in 1948, became governor
            of the state. He served in the office until
            his resignation on December 25, 1952.

            Ricker College was founded and chartered at
            Houlton.

1950   Population: 913,774.

1952   December 26. Burton M. Gross, Republican,
            President of the state senate, became gover-
            nor of Maine. He was previously elected for
            a two-year term beginning January 1953. He
            served in the gubernatorial office until
            January 5, 1955.

1953   WABI-TV, the first television station in
            Maine, began broadcasting from Bangor.

            St. Francis College was established at Bidde-
            ford.

1954   September 13. President Dwight D. Eisenhower
            designated parts of the state disaster areas
            as a result of the damage done by Hurricane
            Edna, September 10-11.

1955   January 5. Edmund S. Muskie, Democrat, who
            had been elected in 1954, became governor
            of the state. He was reelected in 1956 and
            served in the office until his resignation
            on January 3, 1959.

            The state legislature formed the State Depart-
            ment of Economic Development.

1957   September 9. Maine voters chose to change
            the election date in the state from the second
            Monday in September to the first Tuesday in
            November, which was the same date as the rest
            of the nation.

            November. Edmund S. Muskie, governor of the
            state, became the first Democrat to be elected
            by Maine to the United States Senate. Muskie
            resigned on January 3, 1959 as governor of
            the state in order to take his seat in the
            Senate.

1959   January 3. Robert N. Haskell, Republican,
            President of the State Senate, became gover-
            nor of the state upon the resignation of
            Governor Edmund S. Muskie. He served until
            the end of the term on January 8, 1959.

            January 8. Clinton A. Clauson, Democrat, who
            had been elected in 1958, became governor of
            Maine. He served in the office until his
            death on December 30, 1959.

            December 30. John H. Reed, Republican, Presi-
            dent of the State Senate, became governor of
            the state upon the death of Governor Clauson.
            Reed was subsequently elected in a special
            election for the remainder of Clauson's term.
            He was reelected in 1962 and served until
            January 5, 1967.

1960   Population: 969,265

1961   January 31. The state legislature ratified
            the 23rd Amendment to the United States Con-
            stitution.

1963   January 16. The state legislature ratified

the 24th Amendment to the United States Constitution.

November 5. The citizens of the state voted
approval of a constitutional amendment to
increase urban representation in the state
house.

Local school districts were ordered to stop
public school prayers.

Thomas College was founded and chartered at
Waterville.

1964   January 27. Senator Margaret Chase Smith
announced that she would seek the Republican
nomination for President of the United States.

1966   January 24. The state legislature ratified
the 25th Amendment to the United States Constitution.

1967   January 5. Kenneth M. Curtis, Democrat, who
had been elected in 1966, became governor of
the state. He served until January 1, 1975.

1969   Maine adopted personal and corporate income
taxes.

Westbrook College was founded and chartered
at Portland.

1970   Population: 992,048.

November 3. The voters of the state approved
special land use tax schedules.

1971   March 22. When the various routes for "Rail-
pax," (National Railroad Passenger Corporation) were announced, Maine was not on any
of the routes.

April 9. The state legislature ratified the
26th Amendment to the United States Constitution.

1973   November 19. The United States Supreme Court
upheld a Maine law which licensed industries
involved in the handling of oil and imposing
on the licensees liability for any damages
caused by oil spills.

1974   January 18. The state legislature ratified

the Equal Rights Amendment to the United
States Constitution.

November. James B. Longley became the first
individual independent of both major political parties to be elected governor of the
state.

1975   January 1. James B. Longley, Independent,
became governor of the state of Maine.

1976   May 25. Speculators at the New York Mercantile Exchange defaulted on various potato futures contracts when they failed
to meet a 3 p.m. deadline for the deli-
very of nearly 50,000,000 pounds of Maine
potatoes.

November 2. Residents of the state approved a proposition which required deposits on beer and soft-drink containers.

1977   February 28. The United States Justice Department filed a memorandum in the federal
district court in Portland indicating that
it would support the Passamaquoddy and Penobscot Indian tribes in their suit against
the state of Maine for the recovery of their
aboriginal lands. The Indians had made an
agreement to drop their land claims for approximately 60 per cent of the state's
territory if they could receive monetary
compensation.

December 5. The residents of the state repealed the state tax-equalization law which
provided the funds for public education.
The power to tax property was returned to
localities.

BIOGRAPHICAL DIRECTORY

The selected list of governors, United States Senators and Members of the House of Representatives for
Maine, 1820-1977, includes all persons listed in the
CHRONOLOGY for whom basic biographical data was readily
available. Older biographical sources are frequently
in conflict on certain individuals, and in such cases
the source most commonly cited by later authorities
was preferred.

ABBOTT, Nehemiah
Republican
b. Sidney, Maine, March 29, 1804
d. Belfast, Maine, July 26, 1877
U. S. Representative, 1857-59

ALLEN, Amos Lawrence
Republican
b. Waterboro, Maine, March 17, 1837
d. Washington, D. C., February 20, 1911
U. S. Representative, 1899-1911

ALLEN, Elisha Hunt
Whig
b. New Salem, Mass., January 28, 1804
d. Washington, D. C., January 1, 1883
U. S. Representative, 1841-43

AMES, Benjamin
Jefferson Republican
Governor of Louisiana, 1821-22

ANDERSON, Hugh Johnston
Democrat
b. Wiscasset, Maine, May 10, 1801
d. Portland, Ore., May 31, 1881
U. S. Representative, 1837-41
Governor of Louisiana, 1844-47

ANDERSON, John
Jeffersonian Democrat
b. Windham, Maine, July 30, 1792
d. Portland, Maine, August 21, 1853
U. S. Representative, 1825-33

ANDREWS, Charles
Democrat
b. Paris, Maine, February 11, 1814
d. Paris, Maine, April 20, 1852
U. S. Representative, 1851-52

APPLETON, John
Democrat
b. Beverly, Mass., February 11, 1815
d. Portland, Maine, August 22, 1864
U. S. Representative, 1851-53

BAILEY, Jeremiah
    Whig
    b. Little Compton, R. I., May 1, 1773
    d. Wiscasset, Me., July 6, 1853
    U. S. Representative, 1835-37

BARROWS, Lewis O.
    Republicans
    b. Newport, Maine, June 7, 1893
    d. January 30, 1967
    Governor of Maine, 1937-41

BATES, James
    Democrat
    b. Greene, Maine, September 24, 1789
    d. Yarmouth, Maine, February 25, 1882
    U. S. Representative, 1831-33

BAXTER, Percival P.
    Republican
    Governor of Maine, 1921-25

BEEDY, Carroll Lynwood
    Republican
    b. Phillips, Me., August 3, 1880
    d. Washington, D. C., August 30, 1887
    U. S. Representative, 1921-35

BELCHER, Hiram
    Whig
    b. Hallowell, Maine, February 23, 1790
    d. Farmington, Maine, May 6, 1857
    U. S. Representative, 1847-49

BENSON, Samuel Page
    Republican
    b. Winthrop, Maine, November 28, 1804
    d. Yarmouth, Maine, August 12, 1876
    U. S. Representative, 1853-55 (Whig), 1855-57
        (Republican)

BLAINE, James Gillespie
    Republican
    b. West Brownsville, Pa., January 21, 1830
    d. Washington, D. C., January 27, 1893
    U. S. Representative, 1863-76
        Speaker, 1869-75
    U. S. Senator, 1876-81
    U. S. Secretary of State, 1881

BODWELL, Joseph R.
    Republican

d. December 15, 1887
Governor of Louisiana, 1887

BOUTELLE, Charles Addison
    Republican
    b. Damariscotta, Maine, February 9, 1839
    d. Waverley, Mass., May 21, 1901
    U. S. Representative, 1883-1901

BRADBURY, James Ware
    Democrat
    b. Parsonsfield, Me., June 10, 1802
    d. Augusta, Me., January 7, 1901
    U. S. Senator, 1847-53

BRANN, Louis J.
    Democrat
    b. Madison, Maine, July 8, 1876
    d. February 3, 1948
    Governor of Maine, 1933-37

BREWSTER, Ralph Owen
    Republican
    b. Dexter, Maine, February 22, 1888
    d. Boston, Mass., December 25, 1961
    Governor of Maine, 1925-29
    U. S. Representative, 1935-41
    U. S. Senator, 1941-52

BRONSON, David
    Whig
    b. Suffield, Conn., February 8, 1800
    d. St. Michaels, Md., November 30, 1863
    U. S. Representative, 1841-43

BURLEIGH, Edwin Chick
    Republican
    b. Linneus, Maine, November 27, 1843
    d. Augusta, Maine, June 16, 1916
    Governor of Maine, 1889-93
    U. S. Representative, 1897-1911
    U. S. Senator, 1913-16

BURLEIGH, John Holmes
    Republican
    b. South Berwick, Maine, October 9, 1822
    d. South Berwick, Maine, December 5, 1877
    U. S. Representative, 1873-77

BURLEIGH, William
    Adams Democrat
    b. Northwood, N. H., October 24, 1785
    d. South Berwick, Maine, July 2, 1827

U. S. Representative, 1823-27

BUTMAN, Samuel
    b. Worcester, Mass., 1788
    d. Plymouth, Maine, 1827-31
    U. S. Representative, 1827-31

CARTER, Timothy Jarvis
    Democrat
    b. Bethel, in the Maine district of Mass.,
        August 18, 1800
    d. Washington, D. C., March 14, 1848
    U. S. Representative, 1837-38

CARY, Shepard
    Democrat
    b. New Salem, Mass., July 3, 1805
    d. Houlton, Maine, August 9, 1866
    U. S. Representative, 1844-45

CHAMBERLAIN, Joshua L.
    Republican
    b. Brewster, Maine, September 8, 1828
    d. February 24, 1914
    Governor of Maine, 1867-71

CHANDLER, John
    Democrat (Massachusetts - Maine)
    b. Epping, N. H., February 1, 1762
    d. Augusta, Maine, September 25, 1841
    U. S. Representative, 1805-09 (Massachusetts)
    U. S. Senator, 1820-29 (Maine)

CILLEY, Jonathan
    Jackson Democrat
    b. Nottingham, N. H., July 2, 1802
    d. in duel on Marlboro Pike, near Washington,
        D. C., February 24, 1838
    U. S. Representative, 1837-38

CLAPP, Asa William Henry
    Democrat
    b. Portland, Maine, March 6, 1805
    d. Portland, Maine, March 22, 1891
    U. S. Representative, 1847-49

CLARK, Franklin
    Democrat
    b. Wiscasset, Maine, August 2, 1801
    d. Brooklyn, N. Y., August 24, 1874
    U. S. Representative, 1847-49

CLAUSON, Clinton A.
    Democrat
    b. Mitchell, Iowa, March 28, 1895
    d. December 30, 1959
    Governor of Maine, 1959

CLEAVES, Henry B.
    Republican
    b. Bridgton, Maine, February 6, 1840
    d. June 22, 1912
    Governor of Maine, 1893-97

CLIFFORD, Nathan
    Democrat
    b. Rumney, N. H., August 18, 1803
    d. Cornish, Maine, July 25, 1881
    U. S. Representative, 1839-43
    U. S. Attorney General, 1846-48

COBB, William T.
    Republican
    b. Rockland, Maine, July 23, 1857
    d. July 24, 1937
    Governor of Maine, 1905-09

COBURN, Abner
    Republican
    b. Canaan, Maine, March 22, 1803
    d. January 4, 1885
    Governor of Maine, 1863-64

COBURN, Stephen
    Republican
    b. Bloomfield (now Skowhegan), Maine, November
        11, 1817
    d. by drowning at Skowhegan, Maine, July 4,
        1882
    U. S. Representative, 1861

COFFIN, Frank Morey
    Democrat
    b. Lewiston, Maine, July 11, 1919
    U. S. Representative, 1957-61

CONNOR, Selden
    Republican
    b. Fairfield, Maine, January 25, 1839
    d. July 9, 1917
    Governor of Maine, 1876-79

CONY, Samuel
    Republican

        Governor of Maine, 1864-67
CROSBY, William G.
    Whig
    Governor of Maine, 1853-55

CROSS, Burton M.
    Governor of Maine, 1952-55

CURTIS, Kenneth M.
    Democrat
    b. Curtis Corner, Maine, February 8, 1931
    Governor of Maine, 1967-75

CURTIS, Oakley C.
    Democrat
    b. Portland, Maine, March 29, 1865
    d. February 22, 1924
    Governor of Maine, 1915-17

CUSHMAN, Joshua
    Democrat (Massachusetts - Maine)
    b. Halifax, Mass., April 11, 1751
    d. Augusta, Maine, January 27, 1834
    U. S. Representative, 1819-21 (Massachusetts),
        1821-25 (Maine)

CUTLER, Nathan
    Adams Republican
    Governor of Maine, 1829-30

DANA, John W.
    Democrat
    Governor of Maine, 1844, 1847-50

DANA, Judah
    Democrat
    b. Pomfret, Conn., April 25, 1772
    d. Freyburg, Maine, December 27, 1845
    U. S. Senator, 1836-37

DANE, Joseph
    Federalist
    b. Beverly, Mass., October 25, 1778
    d. Kennebunk, Maine, May 1, 1858
    U. S. Representative, 1820-23

DAVEE, Thomas
    Democrat
    b. Plymouth, Mass., December 9, 1797
    d. Blanchard, Maine, December 9, 1841
    U. S. Representative, 1837-41

DAVIS, Daniel F.
    Republican

b. Freedom, Maine, September 12, 1843
d. January 9, 1897
Governor of Maine, 1880-81

DINGLEY, Nelson, Jr.
Republican
b. Durham, Maine, February 15, 1832
d. Washington, D. C., January 13, 1894
Governor of Maine, 1874-76
U. S. Representative, 1881-99

DUNLAP, Robert Pickney
Democrat
b. Brunswick, Maine, August 17, 1794
d. Brunswick, Maine, October 20, 1859
Governor of Maine, 1834-38
U. S. Representative, 1843-47

DUNN, David
Democrat
Governor of Maine, 1844

EVANS, George
b. Hallowell, Maine, January 12, 1797
d. Portland, Maine, April 6, 1867
U. S. Representative, 1829-41
U. S. Senator, 1841-47

FAIRFIELD, John
Democrat
b. Saco, Maine, January 30, 1797
d. Washington, D. C., December 24, 1847
U. S. Representative, 1835-38
Governor of Maine, 1839-43
U. S. Senator, 1843-47

FARLEY, Ephraim Wilder
Whig
b. Newcastle, Maine, August 29, 1817
d. Newcastle, Maine, April 3, 1880
U. S. Representative, 1853-55

FARWELL, Nathan Allen
Republican
b. Unity, Maine, February 24, 1812
d. Rockland, Maine, December 9, 1893
U. S. Senator, 1864-65

FELLOWS, Frank
Republican
b. Bucksport, Maine, November 7, 1889
d. Bangor, Maine, August 27, 1951
U. S. Representative, 1941-51

FERNALD, Bert Manfred
    Republican
    b. West Portland, Maine, April 3, 1858
    d. West Portland, Maine, August 23, 1926
    Governor of Maine, 1909-11
    U. S. Senator, 1916-26

FESSENDEN, Samuel Clement
    Republican
    b. New Gloucester, Maine, March 7, 1815
    d. Stamford, Conn., April 18, 1882
    U. S. Representative, 1861-63

FESSENDEN, Thomas Amory Deblois
    Republican
    b. Portland, Maine, January 23, 1826
    d. Auburn, Maine, September 28, 1868
    U. S. Representative, 1862-63

FESSENDEN, William Pitt
    Whig
    b. Boscawen, N. H., October 16, 1806
    d. Portland, Maine, September 9, 1869
    U. S. Representative, 1841-43
    U. S. Senator, 1854-64, 1865-69

FLYE, Edwin
    Republican
    b. Newcastle, Maine, March 4, 1817
    d. Ashland, Ky., July 12, 1886
    U. S. Representative, 1876-77

FOSTER, Stephen Clark
    Republican
    b. Machias, Maine, December 24, 1799
    d. Pembroke, Maine, October 5, 1872
    U. S. Representative, 1857-61

FRENCH, Ezra Bartlett
    Republican
    b. Landaff, N. H., September 23, 1810
    d. Washington, D. C., April 24, 1880
    U. S. Representative, 1859-61

FRYE, William Pierce
    Republican
    b. Lewiston, Maine, September 2, 1830
    d. Lewiston, Maine, August 8, 1911
    U. S. Representative, 1871-81
    U. S. Senator, 1881-1911
        President pro tempore, 1896-1911

FULLER, Thomas James Duncan
    Democrat
    b. Hardwick, Vt., March 17, 1808
    d. Upperville, Va., February 13, 1876
    U. S. Representative, 1849-57

GARCELON, Alonzo
    b. Maine, 1813
    d. 1906
    Governor of Maine, 1879-80

GARDINER, William T.
    Republican
    b. Newton, Mass., June 12, 1892
    d. August 2, 1953
    Governor of Maine, 1929-33

GARDNER, Obadiah
    Democrat
    b. Grant (formerly Burchville), Mich., September
        13, 1850
    d. Augusta, Maine, July 24, 1938
    U. S. Senator, 1911-13

GARLAND, Peter Adams
    Republican
    b. Boston, Mass., June 16, 1923
    U. S. Representative, 1961-63

GERRY, Elbridge
    Democrat
    b. Waterford, Maine, December 6, 1813
    d. Portland, Maine, April 10, 1886
    U. S. Representative, 1849-51

GILMAN, Charles Jervis
    Republican
    b. Exeter, N. H., February 26, 1824
    d. Brunswick, Maine, February 5, 1901
    U. S. Representative, 1857-59

GOODALL, Louis Bertrand
    Republican
    b. Winchester, N. H., September 23, 1851
    d. Sanford, Maine, June 26, 1935
    U. S. Representative, 1917-21

GOODENOW, Robert
    Whig
    b. Henniker, N. H., April 19, 1800
    d. Farmington, Me., May 15, 1874
    U. S. Representative, 1851-53

GOODENOW, Rufus King
    Whig
    b. Henniker, N. H., April 24, 1790
    d. Paris, Maine, March 24, 1863
    U. S. Representative, 1849-51

GOODWIN, Forrest
    Republican
    b. Skowhegan, Maine, June 14, 1862
    d. Portland, Maine, May 28, 1913
    U. S. Representative, 1913

GOODWIN, John Noble
    Republican (Maine - Arizona)
    b. South Berwick, Maine, October 18, 1824
    d. Paraiso Springs, Calif., April 29, 1887
    U. S. Representative, 1861-63 (Maine)
    Governor of Arizona Territory, 1863-65
    U. S. Representative (Territorial Delegate of
        Arizona), 1865-67

GOULD, Arthur Robinson
    Republican
    b. East Corinth, Maine, March 16, 1857
    d. Presque, Isle, Maine, July 24, 1946
    U. S. Senator, 1926-31

GOULD, Samuel Wadsworth
    Democrat
    b. Porter, Maine, January 1, 1852
    d. Skowhegan, Maine, December 19, 1935
    U. S. Representative, 1911-13

GUERNSEY, Frank Edward
    Republican
    b. Dover, Maine, October 15, 1866
    d. Boston, Mass., January 1, 1927
    U. S. Representative, 1908-17

HAINES, William T.
    Republican
    b. Leuant, Maine, August 7, 1854
    d. June 4, 1919
    Governor of Maine, 1913-15

HALE, Eugene
    Republican
    b. Turner, Maine, June 9, 1836
    d. Washington, D. C., October 28, 1918
    U. S. Representative, 1869-79
    U. S. Senator, 1881-1911

HALE, Frederick
    Republican
    b. Detroit, Mich., October 7, 1874
    d. Portland, Maine, September 28, 1963
    U. S. Senator, 1917-41

HALE, Robert
    Republican
    b. Portland, Maine, November 29, 1889
    U. S. Representative, 1943-59

HALL, Joseph
    Democrat
    b. Methuen, Mass., June 26, 1793
    d. Boston, Mass., December 31, 1859
    U. S. Representative, 1833-37

HALL, Joshua
    Adams Republican
    Acting Governor of Maine, 1830

HAMLIN, Hannibal
    Republican
    b. Paris, Maine, August 27, 1809
    d. Bangor, Maine, July 4, 1891
    U. S. Representative, 1843-47 (Democrat)
    U. S. Senator, 1848-57 (Democrat)
    Governor of Maine, 1857
    U. S. Senator, 1857-61 (Republican)
    Vice President of the United States, 1861-65
    U. S. Senator, 1869-81 (Republican)

HAMLIN, Simon Moulton
    Democrat
    b. Standish (Richville), Maine, August 10, 1866
    d. South Portland, Maine, July 27, 1939
    U. S. Representative, 1935-37

HAMMONS, David
    Democrat
    b. Cornish, Maine, May 12, 1808
    d. Bethel, Maine, November 7, 1888
    U. S. Representative, 1847-49

HARRIS, Mark
    b. Ipswich, Mass., January 27, 1779
    d. New York, N. Y., March 2, 1843
    U. S. Representative, 1822-23

HASKELL, Robert N.
    Republican
    Governor of Maine, 1959

HATHAWAY, William Dodd
    Democrat
    b. Cambridge, Mass., February 21, 1924
    U. S. Representative, 1965-

HERRICK, Ebenezer
    b. Lewiston, Maine, October 21, 1785
    d. Lewiston, Maine, May 7, 1839
    U. S. Representative, 1821-27

HERRICK, Joshua
    Democrat
    b. Beverly, Mass., March 18, 1793
    d. Alfred, Maine, August 30, 1874
    U. S. Representative, 1843-45

HERSEY, Ira Greenlief
    Republican
    b. Hodgdon, Maine, March 31, 1858
    d. Washington, D. C., May 6, 1943
    U. S. Representative, 1917-29

HERSEY, Samuel Freeman
    Republican
    b. Sumner, Maine, April 12, 1812
    d. Bangor, Maine, February 3, 1875
    U. S. Representative, 1873-75

HILDRETH, Horace A.
    Republican
    Governor of Maine, 1945-49

HILL, John F.
    Republican
    b. Eliot, Maine, October 29, 1855
    d. March 16, 1912
    Governor of Maine, 1901-05

HILL, Mark Langdon
    (Massachusetts - Maine)
    b. Biddeford, Maine, June 30, 1772
    d. Phippsburg, Maine, November 26, 1842
    U. S. Representative, 1819-21 (Massachusetts),
        1821-23 (Maine)

HINDS, Asher Crosby
    Republican
    b. Benton, Maine, February 6, 1863
    d. Washington, D. C., May 1, 1919
    U. S. Representative, 1911-17

HOLLAND, Cornelius
    Democrat
    b. Sutton, Mass., July 9, 1783
    d. Canton Point, Maine, June 2, 1870

U. S. Representative, 1830-33

HOLMES, John
    Democrat (Massachusetts - Maine)
    b. Kingston, Mass., March 14, 1773
    d. Portland, Maine, July 7, 1843
    U. S. Representative, 1817-20 (Massachusetts)
    U. S. Senator, 1820-27, 1829-33 (Maine)

HUBBARD, John
    Democrat
    b. March 22, 1794
    d. February 6, 1869
    Governor of Maine, 1850-53

HUNTON, Jonathan G.
    National Republican
    Governor of Maine, 1830-31

JARVIS, Leonard
    Democrat
    b. Boston, Mass., October 19, 1781
    d. Surrey, Maine, October 18, 1854
    U. S. Representative, 1829-37

JOHNSON, Charles Fletcher
    Democrat
    b. Winslow, Maine, February 14, 1859
    d. St. Petersburg, Maine, February 15, 1930
    U. S. Senator, 1911-17

KAVANAGH, Edward
    b. Newcastle, Maine, April 27, 1795
    d. Newcastle, Maine, January 20, 1844
    U. S. Representative, 1831-35
    Governor of Maine, 1843-44

KENT, Edward
    Whig
    b. Concord, N. H., January 8, 1802
    d. May 19, 1877
    Governor of Maine, 1841-42

KIDDER, David
    Whig
    b. December 8, 1787
    d. November 1, 1860
    U. S. Representative, 1823-27

KING, William
    Jeffersonian Republican
    b, Scarborough, Maine, February 9, 1768
    d. June 17, 1852

Governor of Maine, 1820-21

KNOWLTON, Ebenezer
    Republican
    b. December 6, 1815
    d. September 10, 1874
    U. S. Representative, 1855-57

KYROS, Peter N.
    Democrat
    b. Portland, Maine, July 11, 1925
    U. S. Representative, 1967-

LADD, George Washington
    Democrat - Greenbacker
    b. Augusta, Maine, 1818
    d. Bangor, Maine, January 30, 1892
    U. S. Representative, 1879-83

LINCOLN, Enoch
    Adams Republican (Massachusetts - Maine)
    b. Worcester, Mass., December 28, 1788
    d. Augusta, Maine, October 8, 1829
    U. S. Representative, 1818-21 (Massachusetts),
        1821-26 (Maine)
    Governor of Maine, 1827-29

LINDSEY, Stephen Decatur
    Republican
    b. Norridgewock, Maine, March 3, 1828
    d. Norridgewock, Maine, April 26, 1884
    U. S. Representative, 1877-83

LITTLEFIELD, Charles Edgar
    Republican
    b. Lebanon, Maine, June 21, 1851
    d. New York, N. Y., May 2, 1915
    U. S. Representative, 1899-1908

LITTLEFIELD, Nathaniel Swett
    Democrat
    b. Wells, Maine, September 20, 1804
    d. Brighton, Maine, August 15, 1882
    U. S. Representative, 1841-43 (Democrat),
        1849-51 (Cass Democrat)

LONGFELLOW, Stephen
    Federalist
    b. Gorham, Maine, June 23, 1775
    d. Portland, Maine, August 2, 1849
    U. S. Representative, 1823-25

LONGLEY, James B.
    Independent
    b. Lewiston, Maine, April 22, 1924
    Governor of Maine, 1975-

LOWELL, Joshua Adams
    Democrat
    b. Thomaston, Maine, March 20, 1801
    d. East Machias, Maine, March 13, 1874
    U. S. Representative, 1839-43

LYNCH, John
    Republican
    b. Portland, Maine, February 18, 1825
    d. Portland, Maine, July 21, 1892
    U. S. Representative, 1865-73

MACDONALD, Moses
    Democrat
    b. Limerick, Maine, April 8, 1815
    d. Saco, Maine, October 18, 1869
    U. S. Representative, 1851-55

MARBLE, Sebastian S.
    Republican
    Governor of Maine, 1887-89

MARSHALL, Alfred
    Democrat
    b. New Hampshire, 1797
    d. China, Maine, October 2, 1868
    U. S. Representative, 1841-43

MASON, Moses, Jr.
    Democrat
    b. Dublin, N. H., June 2, 1789
    d. Bethel, Maine, June 25, 1868
    U. S. Representative, 1833-37

MAYALL, Samuel
    Democrat
    b. North Gray, Maine, June 21, 1816
    d. St. Paul, Minn., September 17, 1892
    U. S. Representative, 1853-55

MCCRATE, John Dennis
    Democrat
    b. Wiscasset, Maine, October 1, 1802
    d. Sutton, Mass., September 11, 1879
    U. S. Representative, 1845-47

MCGILLICUDDY, Daniel John
    Democrat

    b. Lewiston, Maine, August 27, 1859
    d. Lewiston, Maine, July 30, 1936
    U. S. Representative, 1911-17

MCINTIRE, Clifford Guy
    b. Perham, Maine, May 4, 1908
    U. S. Representative, 1951-65

MCINTIRE, Rufus
    Jackson Democrat
    b. York, Maine, December 19, 1784
    d. Parsonfield, Maine, April 28, 1866
    U. S. Representative, 1827-35

MILLIKEN, Carl E.
    Republican
    b. Pittsfield, Maine, July 13, 1877
    d. May 1, 1961
    Governor of Maine, 1917-21

MILLIKEN, Seth Llewellyn
    Republican
    b. Montville, Maine, December 12, 1831
    d. Washington, D. C., April 18, 1897
    U. S. Representative, 1883-97

MOOR, Wyman Bradbury Seavy
    Democrat
    b. Waterville, Maine, November 11, 1811
    d. Lynchburg, Va., March 10, 1869
    U. S. Senator, 1848

MORAN, Edward Carleton, Jr.
    Democrat
    b. Rockland, Maine, December 29, 1894
    d. Rockland, Maine, July 12, 1967
    U. S. Representative, 1933-37

MORRILL, Anson Peaslee
    Republican
    b. Belgrade, Maine, July 10, 1803
    d. Augusta, Maine, July 4, 1887
    Governor of Maine, 1855-56
    U. S. Representative, 1861-63

MORRILL, Lot Myrick
    Republican
    b. Belgrade, Maine, May 3, 1813
    d. Augusta, Maine, January 10, 1883
    Governor of Maine, 1858-60
    U. S. Senator, 1861-69, 1869-76
    U. S. Secretary of the Treasury, 1876-77

MORRILL, Samuel Plummer
    Republican
    b. Chesterville, Maine, February 11, 1816
    d. Chesterville, Maine, August 4, 1892
    U. S. Representative, 1869-71

MORSE, Freeman Harlow
    Republican
    b. Bath, Maine, February 19, 1807
    d. Surbiton, Surrey, England, February 5, 1891
    U. S. Representative, 1843-45 (Whig),
        1857-61 (Republican)

MARCH, Thompson Henry
    Greenback Labor Reformer
    b. Hampden, Maine, March 29, 1838
    d. Danvers, Mass., December 15, 1886
    U. S. Representative, 1879-83

MUSKIE, Edmund Sixtus
    Democrat
    b. Rumford, Maine, March 28, 1914
    Governor of Maine, 1955-59
    U. S. Senator, 1959-

NELSON, Charles Pembroke
    Republican
    b. Waterville, Maine, July 2, 1907
    d. Augusta, Maine, June 8, 1962
    U. S. Representative, 1949-57

NELSON, John Edward
    Republican
    b. China, Maine, July 12, 1874
    d. Augusta, Maine, April 11, 1955
    U. S. Representative, 1922-23

NOURSE, Amos
    b. Bolton, Mass., December 17, 1794
    d. Bath, Maine, April 7, 1877
    U. S. Senator, 1857

NOYES, Joseph Cobbham
    Whig
    b. Portland, Maine, September 22, 1798
    d. Portland, Maine, July 28, 1868
    U. S. Representative, 1837-39

O'BRIEN, Jeremiah
    Democrat
    b. Machias, Maine, January 21, 1778
    d. Boston, Mass., May 30, 1858
    U. S. Representative, 1823-29

OLIVER, James Churchill
     Democrat
     b. South Portland, Maine, August 6, 1895
     U. S. Representative, 1937-43 (Republican),
          1959-61 (Democrat)

OTIS, John
     Whig
     b. Leeds, Maine, August 3, 1801
     d. Hallowell, Maine, October 17, 1856
     U. S. Representative, 1849-51

PARKHURST, Frederick H.
     Republican
     b. Unity, Maine, November 5, 1864
     d. January 31, 1921
     Governor of Maine, 1921

PARKS, Gorham
     Democrat
     b. Westfield, Mass., May 27, 1794
     d. Bay Ridge, N. Y., November 23, 1877
     U. S. Representative, 1833-37

PARRIS, Albion Keith
     Democrat (Massachusetts - Maine)
     b. Hebron, Maine, January 19, 1788
     d. Portland, Maine, August 26, 1828
     U. S. Representative, 1815-18 (Massachusetts)
     Governor of Maine, 1822-27
     U. S. Senator, 1827-28 (Maine)

PARRIS, Virgil Delphini
     State Rights Democrat
     b. Buckfield, Maine, February 18, 1807
     d. Paris, Maine, June 13, 1874
     U. S. Representative, 1838-41

PARTRIDGE, Donald Barrows
     Republican
     b. Norway, Maine, June 7, 1891
     d. Portland, Maine, June 5, 1946
     U. S. Representative, 1931-33

PAYNE, Frederick George
     Republican
     b. Lewiston, Maine, July 24, 1904
     Governor of Maine, 1949-53
     U. S. Senator, 1953-59

PERHAM, Sidney
     Republican
     b. Woodstock, Maine, March 27, 1819

d. Washington, D. C., April 10, 1907
U. S. Representative, 1863-69
Governor of Maine, 1871-74

PERRY, John Jasiel
Republican
b. Portsmouth, N. H., August 2, 1811
d. Portland, Maine, May 2, 1897
U. S. Representative, 1855-57, 1859-61

PETERS, John Andrew
Republican
b. Ellsworth, Maine, October 9, 1822
d. Bangor, Maine, April 2, 1904
U. S. Representative, 1867-73

PETERS, John Andrew (nephew of the preceding)
Republican
b. Ellsworth, Maine, August 13, 1864
d. Ellsworth, Maine, August 22, 1953
U. S. Representative, 1913-22

PIKE, Frederick Augustus
Republican
b. Calais, Maine, December 9, 1816
d. Calais, Maine, December 2, 1889
U. S. Representative, 1861-69

PLAISTED, Frederick W.
b. Bangor, Maine, July 26, 1865
d, March 4, 1943
Governor of Maine, 1911-13

PLAISTED, Harris Merrill
Republican
b. Jefferson, N. H., November 2, 1828
d. Bangor, Maine, January 31, 1898
U. S. Representative, 1875-77
Governor of Maine, 1881-83

POWERS, Llewellyn
Republican
b. Pittsfield, Maine, October 14, 1836
d. Houlton, Maine, July 28, 1908
U. S. Representative, 1877-79
Governor of Maine, 1896-1900
U. S. Representative, 1901-08

RANDALL, Benjamin
Whig
b. Topsham, Maine, November 14, 1798
d. Bath, Maine, October 11, 1859
U. S. Representative, 1839-43

REED, Isaac
    Whig
    b. Waldboro, Maine, August 22, 1809
    d. Waldboro, Maine, September 19, 1887
    U. S. Representative, 1852-53

REED, John H.
    Republican
    b. Fort Fairfield, Maine, January 25, 1921
    Governor of Maine, 1959-67

REED, Thomas Brackett
    Republican
    b. Portland, Maine, October 18, 1839
    d. Washington, D. C., December 7, 1902
    U. S. Representative, 1877-99
        Speaker, 1889-91, 1895-99

RICE, John Hovey
    b. Mount Vernon, Maine, February 5, 1816
    d. Chicago, Ill., March 14, 1911
    U. S. Representative, 1861-67

RIPLEY, James Wheelock
    Democrat
    b. Hanover, N. H., March 12, 1786
    d. Freyburg, Maine, June 17, 1835
    U. S. Representative, 1826-30

ROBIE, Frederick
    Republican
    b. Gorham, Maine, August 12, 1822
    d. 1912
    Governor of Maine, 1883-87

ROBINSON, Edward
    Whig
    b. Cushing, Maine, November 25, 1796
    d. Thomaston, Maine, February 19, 1857
    U. S. Representative, 1838-39

ROSE, Daniel
    Jeffersonian Republican
    Governor of Maine, 1822

RUGGLES, John
    Democrat
    b. Westboro, Mass., October 8, 1789
    d. Thomaston, Maine, June 20, 1874
    U. S. Senator, 1835-41

SAWTELLE, Cullen
    Democrat

b. Norridgewock, Maine, September 23, 1805
d. Englewood, N. J., November 10, 1887
U. S. Representative, 1845-47, 1849-51

SCAMMAN, John Fairfield
    Democrat
    b. Wells, Maine, October 24, 1786
    d. Saco, Maine, May 22, 1858
    U. S. Representative, 1845-47

SEVERANCE, Luther
    Whig
    b. Montague, Mass., October 26, 1797
    d. Augusta, Maine, January 25, 1855
    U. S. Representative, 1843-47

SEWALL, Sumner
    Republican
    Governor of Maine, 1941-45

SHEPLEY, Ether
    Democrat
    b. Groton, Mass., November 2, 1789
    d. Portland, Maine, January 15, 1877
    U. S. Senator, 1833-36

SMART, Ephraim Knight
    Democrat
    b. Prospect (now Searsport), Maine, September
        3, 1813
    d. Camden, Maine, September 29, 1872
    U. S. Representative, 1847-49, 1851-53

SMITH, Albert
    Democrat
    b. Hanover, Mass., January 3, 1793
    d. Boston, Mass., May 29, 1872
    U. S. Representative, 1839-41

SMITH, Clyde Harold
    Republican
    b. near Harmony, Maine, June 9, 1876
    d. Washington, D. C., April 8, 1940
    U. S. Representative, 1937-40

SMITH, Francis Ormand Jonathan
    Democrat
    b. Brentwood, N. H., November 23, 1806
    d, Deering (later Woodfords), Maine, October
        14, 1876
    U. S. Representative, 1833-39

SMITH, Margaret Chase
    Republican
    b. Skowhegan, Maine, December 14, 1897
    U. S. Representative, 1940-49
    U. S. Senator, 1949-73

SMITH, Samuel E.
    Jackson Democrat
    Governor of Maine, 1831-34

SNOW, Donald Francis
    Republican
    b. Bangor, Maine, September 6, 1877
    d. Gorham, Maine, February 12, 1958
    U. S. Representative, 1929-33

SOMES, Daniel Eton
    Republican
    b. Meredith (now Laconia), N. H., May 20, 1815
    d. Washington, D. C., February 13, 1888
    U. S. Representative, 1859-61

SPRAGUE, Peleg
    National Republican
    b. Duxbury, Mass., April 27, 1793
    d. Boston, Mass., October 13, 1880
    U. S. Representative, 1825-29
    U. S. Senator, 1829-35

STETSON, Charles
    Democrat
    b. New Ipswich, N. H., November 2, 1801
    d. Bangor, Maine, March 27, 1863
    U. S. Representative, 1849-51

SWASEY, John Philip
    Republican
    b. Canton, Maine, September 4, 1839
    d. Canton, Maine, May 27, 1928
    U. S. Representative, 1908-11

SWEAT, Lorenzo De Medici
    Democrat
    b. Parsonsfield, Maine, May 26, 1818
    d. Portland, Maine, July 26, 1898
    U. S. Representative, 1863-65

TUPPER, Stanley R.
    Republican
    b. Boothbay Harbor, Maine, January 25, 1921
    U. S. Representative, 1961-67

UTTERBECK, John Gregg
    Democrat
    b. Franklin, Ind., July 12, 1872
    d. Bangor, Maine, July 11, 1955
    U. S. Representative, 1933-35

VOSE, Richard H.
    Governor of Maine, 1841

WALTON, Charles Wesley
    Republican
    b. Mexico, Maine, December 9, 1819
    d. Portland, Maine, January 24, 1900
    U. S. Representative, 1861-62

WASHBURN, Israel, Jr.
    Republican
    b. Livermore, Maine, June 6, 1813
    d. Philadelphia, Pa., May 12, 1883
    U. S. Representative, 1851-55 (Whig)
        1855-61 (Republican)
    Governor of Maine, 1861-62

WELLS, Samuel
    Democrat
    Governor of Maine, 1856-57

WHITE, Benjamin
    Democrat
    b. Goshen (now Vienna), Maine, May 13, 1790
    d. Montville, Maine, June 7, 1860
    U. S. Representative, 1843-45

WHITE, Wallace Humphrey, Jr.
    Republican
    b. Lewiston, Maine, August 6, 1877
    d. Auburn, Maine, March 31, 1952
    U. S. Representative, 1817-31
    U. S. Senator, 1831-49

WHITMAN, Ezekiel
    Federalist (Massachusetts - Maine)
    b. East Bridgewater, Mass., March 9, 1776
    d. East Bridgewater, Mass., August 1, 1866
    U. S. Representative, 1809-11, 1817-21 (Massa-
        chusetts), 1821-22 (Maine)

WILEY, James Sullivan
    Democrat
    b. Mercer, Maine, January 22, 1808
    d. Fryeburg, Me., December 21, 1891
    U. S. Representative, 1847-49

WILLIAMS, Hezekiah
        b. near Woodstock, Vt., July 28, 1798
        d. Castine, Maine, October 23, 1856
        U. S. Representative, 1945-49

WILLIAMS, Joseph H.
        Republican
        Governor of Maine, 1857-58

WILLIAMS, Revel
        Democrat
        b. Hallowell, Maine, June 2, 1783
        d. Augusta, Maine, July 25, 1862
        U. S. Senator, 1837-43

WILLIAMSON, William Durkee
        Democrat
        b. Canterbury, Conn., July 31, 1779
        d. Bangor, Maine, May 27, 1846
        Governor of Maine, 1821
        U. S. Representative, 1821-23

WINGATE, Joseph Ferdinand
        Democrat
        b. Haverhill, Maine, June 29, 1786
        d. South Windsor, Maine
        U. S. Representative, 1827-31

WOOD, John M.
        Republican
        b. Minisink, N. Y., November 17, 1813
        d. Boston, Mass., December 24, 1864
        U. S. Representative, 1855-59

PROMINENT PERSONALITIES

The following select list of prominent persons of Maine has been selected to indicate the valuable contributions they have made to American life.

COPLEY, John Singleton
    b. Boston, Mass., 1738
    d. London, England, September 9, 1815
    Painted portraits of John Adams, Samuel Adams,
        the Earl of Mansfield

CURTIS, Cyrus H.
    b. Portland, Me., June 18, 1850
    d. June 7, 1933
    Established Ladies' Home Journal, 1876
    Head of Curtis Publishing Company
    Also published The Country Gentleman and
        The Saturday Evening Post
    Purchased The Public Ledger, 1913
    Purchased New York Evening Post, 1923

DIX, Dorothea Lynde
    b. Hampden, Me., April 4, 1802
    d. July 17, 1887
    Established and headed school for girls, 1820-
        35
    Achieved reforms in treatment of the insane
        in prisons, almhouses and houses of
        correction in Massachusetts and in
        other states from 1841 on
    Served during Civil War as superintendent
        of women nurses

DOW, Neal
    b. Portland, Me., March 20, 1804
    d. October 2, 1897
    Mayor of Portland, 1851
    Drafted prohibition law, submitted it to state
        legislature and helped to achieve its
        passage
    Candidate of Prohibition Party for President
        of the U. S., 1880

ECKSTROM, Fannie Hardy
    b. Brewer, Me., June 18, 1865
    d. December 31, 1946
    Co-founder of Folk-Song Society of the Northeast

Author: The Penobscot Man, 1904
        Handicrafts of the Modern Indians of
            Maine, 1932
        Old John Neptune and Other Maine Indian
            Shamans, 1945

FULLER, Melville Weston
    b. Augusta, Me., February 11, 1833
    d. 1910
    Chief Justice U. S. Supreme Court, 1888-1910
    Member, Permanent Court of Arbitration, 1900-
        10

KING, Rufus
    b. New York, N. Y., january 26, 1814
    d. October 13, 1876
    Adjutant General, New York State, 1839-43
    Part owner Milwaukee Sentinel and Gazette, 1845-47
        editor, 1845-61
    U. S. Minister to Rome, 1861, 1863-68

LITTLEDALE, Clara S.
    b. Belfast, Me., January 31, 1891
    d. January 9, 1956
    Reporter and editor for New York Evening Post,
        1913-14
    Free lance writer, 1919-26
    Editor, Parents' Magazine, 1926-56

MAXIM, Sir Hiram Stevens
    b. Sangerville, Me., February 5, 1840
    d. November 24, 1916
    Went to England, 1881
    Patented various electrical inventions including
        incandescent lamps
    Invented Maxim Gun, automatic weapon
    Knighted by Queen Victoria, 1901

MAXIM, Hudson
    b. Orneville County, Me., February 3, 1853
    d. May 6, 1927
    First to make smokeless powder in U. S.
    Built factory to manufacture dynamite and
        smokeless powder at Maxim, N. J., 1890

MUNSEY, Frank Andrew
    b. Mercer, Me., August 21, 1854
    d. December 22, 1925
    Publisher of New York Evening Sun and Evening
        Telegram, Munsey's Magazine, and Argosy
        All-Story Weekly

POOR, Henry Varnum
    b. Andover, Me., 1812
    d. 1905
    Editor, <u>American Railroad Journal</u>, 1849-62

PUTNAM, George Palmer
    b. Brunswick, Me., February 7, 1814
    d. December 20, 1872
    Ran store selling American books, London,
        England, 1841-48
    Started book publishing company, G. P. Putnam
        & Son, 1866 - Became G. P. Putnam & Sons,
        1871
    Founder and publisher of <u>Putnam's Monthly</u>
        <u>Magazine</u>, 1853-57, 1868-70

RASLE, Sebastian
    b. France, 1657
    d. Norridgecock, Me., 1724
    Jesuit Missionary assigned to Norridgecock,
        Me., Indian village, where he made
        converts.
    Constructed chapel and taught Christian
        principles
    Killed when English attacked village

WEYMOUTH, George
    b. 1570 ?
    d. 1613 ?
    English explorer and adventurer
    Sent on voyage supposedly to discover northwest
        passage, actually to secure England's
        claime to the New World, 1605
    Explored Maine coast, traded with Indians
    Brought 5 Indians to England

FIRST STATE CONSTITUTION

CONSTITUTION OF THE STATE OF MAINE—1819 * ª

PREAMBLE

We, the people of Maine, in order to establish justice, insure tranquility, provide for our mutual defence, promote our common welfare, and secure to ourselves and our posterity the blessings of liberty, acknowledging with grateful hearts the goodness of the Sovereign Ruler of the Universe in affording us an opportunity, so favorable to the design; and, imploring His aid and direction in its accomplishment, do agree to form ourselves into a free and independent State, by the style and title of the STATE OF MAINE, and do ordain and establish the following constitution for the government of the same.

ARTICLE I

DECLARATION OF RIGHTS

SECTION 1. All men are born equally free and independent, and have certain natural, inherent and unalienable rights, among which are those of enjoying and defending life and liberty, acquiring, possessing and protecting property, and of pursuing and obtaining safety and happiness.

SEC. 2. All power is inherent in the people; all free governments are founded in their authority and instituted for their benefit; they have therefore an unalienable and indefeasible right to institute government, and to alter, reform, or totally change the same, when their safety and happiness require it.

---

* Verified from " The Constitution of the State of Maine, formed in Convention at Portland, October twenty-ninth, and adopted by the People in town meetings, on the sixth day of December, A. D. 1819, and of the Independence of the United States the Forty-fourth, together with Amendments subsequently made thereto, and arranged, as amended, in pursuance of a Resolve of the Legislature approved February twenty-fourth, A. D. 1875, with Amendments adopted since the last named date with notes on the Declaration of Rights. By L. D. Carver. Augusta: Kennebec Journal Print. 1902." 62 pp.

ª Formed in Convention at Portland, October 29, and adopted by the People in Town Meetings, December 6, A. D. 1819, and of the Independence of the United States the Forty-fourth, together with the XXI Amendments Subsequently made Thereto, Arranged, as Amended, in pursuance of a Legislative Resolve of February 24, 1875, by the Chief Justice of the Supreme Judicial Court, the Honorable John Appleton, whose draft and arrangement was, by a Resolve of February 23, 1876, approved by the Legislature, and ordered to be enrolled on parchment and to be deposited in the office of the Secretary of State as " the Supreme Law of the State."

[NOTE.—By Resolve of January 12, 1875, Governor Dingley was authorized to appoint a Commission of ten persons, " to consider and frame such amendments to the Constitution of Maine as may seem necessary, to be reported to the Legislature;" and Edward Kent, William P. Haines, George F. Talbot, William M. Rust, Henry E. Robins, Washington Gilbert, James C. Madigan, Artemas Libbey, Frederick A. Pike and William K. Kimball, were appointed.

Nine of the amendments reported by the Commission, viz.:—in relation to (XIII) Election of Senators by Plurality vote; (XIV) Special Legislation and Corporations; (XV) Power of Governor to pardon; (XVI) Appointment of Judges of Municipal and Police Courts; (XVII) Taxation; (XVIII) Abolishing the Land Agency; (XIX) Constitutional Conventions; (XX) Bribery at Elections; (XXI) Codification of the Amended Constitution; were submitted to the people by a Resolve of February 24, 1875; and adopted at the annual election, September 13, 1875.]

Sec. 3. All men have a natural and unalienable right to worship Almighty God according to the dictates of their own consciences, and no one shall be hurt, molested or restrained in his person, liberty or estate for worshiping God in the manner and season most agreeable to the dictates of his own conscience, nor for his religious professions or sentiments, provided he does not disturb the public peace, nor obstruct others in their religious worship;—and all persons demeaning themselves peaceably as good members of the State shall be equally under the protection of the laws, and no subordination nor preference of any one sect or denomination to another shall ever be established by law, nor shall any religious test be required as a qualification for any office or trust, under this State; and all religious societies in this State, whether incorporate or unincorporate, shall at all times have the exclusive right of electing their public teachers, and contracting with them for their support and maintenance.

Sec. 4. Every citizen may freely speak, write and publish his sentiments on any subject, being responsible for the abuse of this liberty; no laws shall be passed regulating or restraining the freedom of the press; and in prosecutions for any publication respecting the official conduct of men in public capacity, or the qualifications of those who are candidates for the suffrages of the people, or where the matter published is proper for public information, the truth thereof may be given in evidence, and in all indictments for libels, the Jury, after having received the direction of the Court, shall have a right to determine, at their discretion, the law and the fact.

Sec. 5. The people shall be secure in their persons, houses, papers and possessions from all unreasonable searches and seizures; and no warrant to search any place, or seize any person or thing, shall issue without a special designation of the place to be searched, and the person or thing to be seized, nor without probable cause—supported by oath or affirmation.

Sec. 6. In all criminal prosecutions, the accused shall have a right to be heard by himself and his counsel, or either, at his election;

To demand the nature and cause of the accusation, and have a copy thereof;

To be confronted by the witnesses against him;

To have compulsory process for obtaining witnesses in his favor;

To have a speedy, public and impartial trial, and, except in trials by martial law or impeachment, by a jury of the vicinity. He shall not be compelled to furnish or give evidence against himself, nor be deprived of his life, liberty, property or privileges, but by judgment of his peers, or by the law of the land.

Sec. 7. No person shall be held to answer for a capital or infamous crime, unless on a presentment or indictment of a grand jury, except in cases of impeachment, or in such cases of offences as are usually cognizable by a justice of the peace, or in cases arising in the army or navy, or in the militia when in actual service in time of war or public danger. The Legislature shall provide by law a suitable and impartial mode of selecting juries and their usual number and unanimity, in indictments and convictions, shall be held indispensable.

Sec. 8. No person, for the same offence, shall be twice put in jeopardy of life or limb.

Sec. 9. Sanguinary laws shall not be passed: all penalties and punishments shall be proportioned to the offence; excessive bail shall not be required, nor excessive fines imposed, nor cruel nor unusual punishments inflicted.

SEC. 10. No person before conviction shall be bailable for any of the crimes, which now are, or have been denominated capital offences since the adoption of the Constitution, where the proof is evident or the presumption great, whatever the punishment of the crimes may be. And the privilege of the writ of habeas corpus shall not be suspended, unless when in case of rebellion or invasion the public safety may require it.

SEC. 11. The Legislature shall pass no bill of attainder, ex post facto law, nor law impairing the obligation of contracts, and no attainder shall work corruption of blood nor forfeiture of estate.

SEC. 12. Treason against this State shall consist only in levying war against it, adhering to its enemies, giving them aid and comfort. No person shall be convicted of treason unless on the testimony of two witnesses to the same overt act, or confession in open court.

SEC. 13. The laws shall not be suspended but by the Legislature or its authority.

SEC. 14. No person shall be subject to corporal punishment under military law, except such as are employed in the army or navy, or in the militia when in actual service in time of war or public danger.

SEC. 15. The people have a right at all times in an orderly and peaceable manner to assemble to consult upon the common good, to give instructions to their representatives, and to request, of either department of the government by petition or remonstrance, redress of their wrongs and grievances.

SEC. 16. Every citizen has a right to keep and bear arms for the common defence; and this right shall never be questioned.

SEC. 17. No standing army shall be kept up in time of peace without the consent of the Legislature, and the military shall, in all cases, and at all times, be in strict subordination to the civil power.

SEC. 18. No soldier shall, in time of peace, be quartered in any house without the consent of the owner or occupant, nor in time of war, but in a manner to be prescribed by law.

SEC. 19. Every person, for an injury done him in his person, reputation, property or immunities, shall have remedy by due course of law; and right and justice shall be administered freely and without sale, completely and without denial, promptly and without delay.

SEC. 20. In all civil suits, and in all controversies concerning property, the parties shall have a right to a trial by jury, except in cases where it has heretofore been otherwise practiced; the party claiming the right may be heard by himself and his counsel, or either, at his election.

SEC. 21. Private property shall not be taken for public uses without just compensation; nor unless the public exigencies require it.

SEC. 22. No tax or duty shall be imposed without the consent of the people or of their representatives in the Legislature.

SEC. 23. No title of nobility or hereditary distinction, privilege, honor or emolument, shall ever be granted or confirmed, nor shall any office be created, the appointment to which shall be for a longer time than during good behavior.

SEC. 24. The enumeration of certain rights shall not impair nor deny others retained by the people.

ARTICLE II

ELECTORS

SEC. 1. Every male citizen of the United States of the age of twenty-one years and upwards, excepting paupers, persons under guardianship, and Indians not taxed, having his residence established in this State for the term of three months next preceding any election, shall be an elector for Governor, Senators and Representatives, in the town or plantation where his residence is so established; and the elections shall be by written ballot. But persons in the military, naval or marine service of the United States, or this State, shall not be considered as having obtained such established residence by being stationed in any garrison, barrack, or military place, in any town or plantation; nor shall the residence of a student at any seminary of learning entitle him to the right of suffrage in the town or plantation where such seminary is established. No person, however, shall be deemed to have lost his residence by reason of his absence from the State in the military service of the United States, or of this State.

SEC. 2. Electors shall, in all cases, except treason, felony or breach of the peace, be privileged from arrest on the days of election, during their attendance at, going to, and returning therefrom.

SEC. 3. No elector shall be obliged to do duty in the militia on any day of election, except in time of war or public danger.

SEC. 4. The election of Governor, Senators and Representatives shall be on the second Monday of September *annually* forever. But citizens of the State absent therefrom in the military service of the United States or of this State, and not in the regular army of the United States, being otherwise qualified electors, shall be allowed to *vote on Tuesday next after the first Monday of November, in the year of our Lord one thousand eight hundred and sixty-four, for governor and senators, and their votes shall be counted and allowed in the same manner, and with the same effect, as if given the second Monday of September in that year. And they shall be allowed to vote* for governor, senators and representatives on the second Monday of September *annually thereafter forever*, in the manner herein provided. On the day of election a poll shall be opened at every place without this State where a regiment, battalion, battery, company, or detachment of not less than twenty soldiers from the State of Maine, may be found or stationed, and every citizen of said State of the age of twenty-one years, in such military service, shall be entitled to vote as aforesaid; and he shall be considered as voting in the city, town, plantation and county in this State where he resided when he entered the service. The vote shall be taken by regiments when it can conveniently be done; when not so convenient, any detachment or part of a regiment not less than twenty in number, and any battery or part thereof numbering twenty or more, shall be entitled to vote wherever they may be. The three ranking officers of such regiment, battalion, battery, company, or part of either, as the case may be, acting as such on the day of election, shall be supervisors of elections. If no officers, then three non-commissioned officers according to their seniority shall be such supervisors. If any officer or non-commissioned officer shall neglect or refuse to act, the next in rank shall take his place. In case there are no officers or non-commissioned officers present, or if they or either of them refuse to act, the electors present, not less than twenty, may choose, by written ballot enough of their own number, not exceeding three, to fill the vacancies, and the persons so chosen shall be supervisors of elections. All supervisors shall be first sworn to support the constitution of the United States and of this State, and faithfully and impartially to perform the duties of supervisors of elections. Each is authorized to administer the necessary oath to the others; and certificates thereof shall be annexed to the lists of votes by them to be made and returned into the office of the secretary of state of this State as hereinafter provided. The polls shall be opened and closed at such hours as the supervisors, or a majority of them, shall direct; *provided however*, that due notice and sufficient time shall be given for all voters in the regiment, battalion, battery, detachment, company, or part of either, as the case may be, to vote. Regimental and field officers shall be entitled to vote with their respective commands. When not in actual command, such officers, and also all general and staff officers and all surgeons, assistant surgeons, and chaplains, shall be entitled to vote at any place where polls are opened. The supervisors of elections shall prepare a ballot box or other suitable receptacle for the ballots. Upon one side of every ballot shall be printed or written the name of the county, and also of the city, town or plantation of this State, in which is the residence of the person proposing to vote. Upon the other side shall be the name or names of the persons to be voted for, and the office or offices which he or they are intended to fill. And before receiving any vote, the supervisors, or a majority of them, must be satisfied of the age and citizenship of the person claiming to vote, and that he has in fact a residence in the county, city, town or plantation which is printed or written on the vote offered by him. If his right to vote is challenged, they may require him to make true answers, upon oath, to all interrogatories touching his age, citizenship, residence, and right to vote, and shall hear any other evidence offered by him, or by those who challenge his right. They shall keep correct poll-lists of the names of all persons allowed to vote, and of their respective places of residence in this State, and also the number of the regiment and company or battery to which they belong; which lists shall be certified by them or by a majority of them, to be correct, and that such residence is in accordance with the indorsement of the residence of each voter on his vote. They shall check the name of every person before he is allow to vote, and the check-mark shall be plainly made against his name on the poll-lists. They shall sort, count and publicly declare the votes at the head of their respective commands on the day of election, unless prevented by the public enemy, and in that case as soon thereafter as may be; and on the same day of said declaration they shall form a list of the persons voted for, with the number of votes for each person against his name, and the office which he was intended to fill, and shall sign and seal up such list and cause the same, together with the poll-lists aforesaid, to be delivered into the office of the secretary of state aforesaid, *on or before the first day of December, in the year one thousand eight hundred and sixty-four and* on or before the fifteenth day of November *annually thereafter forever.* The legislature of this State may pass any law additional to the foregoing provisions, if any shall, in practice, be found necessary in order more fully to carry into effect the purpose thereof.

ARTICLE III

DISTRIBUTION OF POWERS

SEC. 1. The powers of this government shall be divided into three distinct departments, the Legislative, Executive and Judicial.

SEC. 2. No person or persons, belonging to one of these departments, shall exercise any of the powers properly belonging to either of the others, except in the cases herein expressly directed or permitted.

ARTICLE IV.—PART FIRST

LEGISLATIVE POWER.—HOUSE OF REPRESENTATIVES

SEC. 1. The legislative power shall be vested in two distinct branches, a House of Representatives, and a Senate, each to have a negative on the other, and both to be styled the Legislature of Maine and the style of their acts and laws shall be, " BE IT ENACTED BY THE SENATE AND HOUSE OF REPRESENTATIVES, IN LEGISLATURE ASSEMBLED."

SEC. 2. The House of Representatives shall consist of one hundred and fifty-one members, to be elected by the qualified electors, for *one year* from the day next preceding the *annual meeting* of the Legislature. The Legislature, *which shall first be convened under this Constitution,* shall, *on or before the fifteenth day of August, in the year of our Lord, one thousand eight hundred and twenty-one, and the Legislature,* within every *subsequent* period of at most ten years, and at least five, cause the number of the inhabitants of the State to be ascertained, exclusive of foreigners not naturalized and Indians not taxed. The number of Representatives shall, at the several periods of making such enumeration, be fixed and apportioned among the several counties as near as may be, according to the number of inhabitants, having regard to the relative increase of population. *The number of representatives shall, on said first apportionment, be not less than one hundred nor more than one hundred and fifty.*

SEC. 3. Each town having fifteen hundred inhabitants may elect one representative; each town having three thousand seven hundred and fifty may elect two; each town having six thousand seven hundred and fifty may elect three; each town having ten thousand five hundred may elect four; each town having fifteen thousand may elect five; each town having twenty thousand two hundred and fifty may elect six; each town having twenty-six thousand two hundred and fifty may elect seven; but no town shall ever be entitled to more than seven representatives; and towns and plantations duly organized, not having fifteen hundred inhabitants, shall be classed, as conveniently as may be, into districts containing that number, and so as not to divide towns; and each such district may elect one representative; *and, when on this apportionment the number of representatives shall be two hundred, a different apportionment shall take place upon the above principle;* and, in case the fifteen hundred shall be too large or too small to apportion all the representatives to any county, it shall be so increased or diminished as to give the number of representatives according to the above rule and proportion; and whenever any town or towns, plantation or plantations not entitled to elect a representative shall determine against a classification with any other town or plantation, the Legislature may, at each apportionment of representatives, on the application of such town or plantation, authorize it to elect a representative for such portion of time and such periods, as shall be equal to its portion of representation; and the right of representation, so established, shall not be altered until the next general apportionment.

Sec. 4. No person shall be a member of the House of Representatives, unless he shall, at the commencement of the period for which he is elected, have been five years a citizen of the United States, have arrived at the age of twenty-one years, have been a resident in this State one year, *or from the adoption of this constitution;* and for the three months next preceding the time of his election shall have been, and, during the period for which he is elected, shall continue to be a resident in the town or district which he represents.

Sec. 5. The meetings within this State for the choice of representatives shall be warned in due course of law by the selectmen of the several towns seven days at least before the election, and the selectmen thereof shall preside impartially at such meetings, receive the votes of all the qualified electors present, sort, count and declare them in open town meeting, and in the presence of the town clerk, who shall form a list of the persons voted for, with the number of votes for each person against his name, shall make a fair record thereof in the presence of the selectmen and in open town meeting. And the towns and plantations organized by law, belonging to any class herein provided, shall hold their meetings at the same time in the respective towns and plantations; and the town and plantation meetings in such towns and plantations shall be notified, held and regulated, the votes received, sorted, counted and declared in the same manner. And the assessors and clerks of plantations shall have all the powers, and be subject to all the duties, which selectmen and town clerks have, and are subject to by this Constitution. And fair copies of the lists of votes shall be attested by the selectmen and town clerks of towns, and the assessors of plantations, and sealed up in open town and plantation meetings; and the town and plantation clerks respectively shall cause the same to be delivered into the secretary's office thirty days at least before the first Wednesday of January *annually.* And the governor and council shall examine the returned copies of such lists, and also all lists of votes of citizens in the military service, returned to the secretary's office, as provided in article second, section four, of this Constitution; and twenty days before the said first Wednesday of January, *annually,* shall issue a summons to such persons as shall appear to be elected by a plurality of all the votes returned, to attend and take their seats. But all such lists shall be laid before the House of Representatives on the first Wednesday of January *annually,* and

they shall finally determine who are elected. The electors resident in
any city may, at any meeting duly notified for the choice of representatives vote for such representatives in their respective ward meetings,
and the wardens in said wards shall preside impartially at such meetings, receive the votes of all qualified electors present, sort, count and
declare them in open ward meetings, and in the presence of the ward
clerk, who shall form a list of the persons voted for, with the number
of votes for each person against his name, shall make a fair record
thereof in the presence of the warden, and in open ward meetings;
and a fair copy of this list shall be attested by the warden and ward
clerk, sealed up in open ward meeting, and delivered to the city clerk
within twenty-four hours after the close of the polls. And the electors resident in any city may at any meetings duly notified and holden
for the choice of any other civil officers for whom they have been
required heretofore to vote in town meeting, vote for such officers in
their respective wards, and the same proceedings shall be had by the
warden and ward clerk in each ward, as in the case of votes for representatives. And the aldermen of any city shall be in session within
twenty-four hours after the close of the polls in such meetings, and in
the presence of the city clerk shall open, examine and compare the
copies from the lists of votes given in the several wards, of which the
city clerk shall make a record, and return therof shall be made into
the Secretary of State's office in the same manner as selectmen of
towns are required to do.

SEC. 6. Whenever the seat of a member shall be vacated by death,
resignation, or otherwise, the vacancy may be filled by a new election.

SEC. 7. The House of Representatives shall choose their speaker,
clerk and other officers.

SEC. 8. The House of Representatives shall have the sole power of
impeachment.

ARTICLE IV.—PART SECOND

SENATE

SEC. 1. The Senate shall consist of *not less than twenty nor more
than* thirty-one members, elected at the same time, and for the same
term, as the representatives, by the qualified electors of the district
into which the State shall from time to time be divided.

SEC. 2. The Legislature, *which shall be first convened under this
Constitution,* shall, *on or before the fifteenth day of August in the
year of our Lord, one thousand eight hundred and twenty-one, and
the Legislature at every subsequent period of* ten years, cause the
State to be divided into districts for the choice of senators. The districts shall conform, as near as may be, to county lines, and be apportioned according to the number of inhabitants. The number of senators shall *not exceed twenty at the first apportionment, and shall at
each apportionment be increased, until they shall amount to thirty-
one, according to the increase in the House of Representatives.*

SEC. 3. The meetings within this state for the election of senators
shall be notified, held and regulated, and the votes received, sorted,
counted, declared and recorded, in the same manner as those for
representatives. And fair copies of the list of votes shall be attested
by the selectmen and town clerks of towns, and the assessors and

clerks of plantations, and sealed up in open town and plantation meetings; and the town and plantation clerks respectively shall cause the same to be delivered into the secretary's office thirty days at least before the first Wednesday of January. All other qualified electors, living in places unincorporated, who shall be assessed to the support of the government by the assessors of an adjacent town, shall have the privilege of voting for senators, representatives and governor in such town; and shall be notified by the selectmen thereof for that purpose accordingly.

SEC. 4. The Governor and Council shall, as soon as may be, examine the returned copies of such lists, and also the lists of votes-of-citizens in the military service, returned into the secretary's office, and twenty days before the said first Wednesday of January, issue a summons to such persons, as shall appear to be elected by a plurality of the votes for each district, to attend that day and take their seats.

SEC. 5. The Senate shall, on the said first Wednesday of January, *annually*, determine who are elected by a plurality of votes to be senators in each district; and in case the full number of senators to be elected from each district shall not have been so elected, the members of the house of representatives and such senators, as shall have been elected, shall from the highest numbers of the persons voted for, on said lists, equal to twice the number of senators deficient, in every district, if there be so many voted for, elect by joint ballot the number of senators required; and in this manner all vacancies in the Senate shall be supplied as soon as may be, after such vacancies happen.

SEC. 6. The senators shall be twenty-five years of age at the commencement of the term, for which they are elected, and in all other respects their qualifications shall be the same, as those of the representatives.

SEC. 7. The Senate shall have the sole power to try all impeachments, and when sitting for that purpose shall be on oath or affirmation, and no person shall be convicted without the concurrence of two-thirds of the members present. Their judgment, however, shall not extend farther than to removal from office, and disqualification to hold or enjoy any office of honor, trust or profit under this State. But the party, whether convicted or acquitted, shall nevertheless be liable to indictment, trial, judgment and punishment according to law.

SEC. 8. The Senate shall choose their president, secretary and other officers.

ARTICLE IV.—PART THIRD

LEGISLATIVE POWER

SEC. 1. The Legislature shall convene on the first Wednesday of January, *annually*, and shall have full power to make and establish all reasonable laws and regulations for the defence and benefit of the people of this State, not repugnant to this Constitution, nor to that of the United States.

SEC. 2. Every bill or resolution having the force of law, to which the concurrence of both houses may be necessary, except on a question of adjournment, which shall have passed both houses, shall be presented to the Governor, and if he approve, he shall sign it; if not, he shall return it with his objections to the house, in which it shall have originated, which shall enter the objections at large on its journals, and proceed to reconsider it. If after such reconsideration, two-thirds of that house shall agree to pass it, it shall be sent together with the objections, to the other house by which it shall be reconsidered, and, if aproved by two-thirds of that house, it shall have the same effect, as if it had been signed by the Governor; but in all such cases, the votes of both houses shall be taken by yeas and nays, and the names of the persons, voting for and against the bill or resolution, shall be entered on the journals of both houses respectively. If the bill or resolution shall not be returned by the Governor within five days (Sundays excepted) after it shall have been presented to him, it shall have the same force and effect, as if he had signed it, unless the Legislature, by their adjournment prevent its return, in which case it shall have such force and effect, unless returned within three days after their next meeting.

SEC. 3. Each house shall be the judge of the elections and qualifications of its own members, and a majority shall constitute a quorum to do business; but a smaller number may adjourn from day to day, and may compel the attendance of absent members, in such manner, and under such penalties as each house shall provide.

SEC. 4. Each house may determine the rules of its proceedings, punish its members for disorderly behavior, and, with the concurrence of two-thirds, expel a member, but not a second time for the same cause.

SEC. 5. Each house shall keep a journal, and from time to time publish its proceedings, except such parts as in their judgment may require secrecy; and the yeas and nays of the members of either house on any question, shall, at the desire of one-fifth of those present, be entered on the journals.

SEC. 6. Each house, during its session, may punish by imprisonment any person, not a member, for disrespectful or disorderly behavior in its presence, for obstructing any of its proceedings, threatening, assaulting or abusing any of its members for anything said, done, or doing in either house; *provided*, that no imprisonment shall extend beyond the period of the same session.

SEC. 7. The senators and representatives shall receive such compensation, as shall be established by law; but no law increasing their compensation shall take effect during the existence of the Legislature which enacted it. The expenses of the House of Representatives in travelling to the Legislature and returning therefrom, once in each session and no more, shall be paid by the State out of the public treasury to every member, who shall seasonably attend, in the judgment of the house, and does not depart therefrom without leave.

SEC. 8. The senators and representatives shall, in all cases except treason, felony or breach of the peace, be privileged from arrest during their attendance at, going to, and returning from each session of the Legislature; and no member shall be liable to answer for anything spoken in debate in either house, in any court or place elsewhere.

SEC. 9. Bills, orders or resolutions, may originate in either house, and may be altered, amended or rejected in the other; but all bills for raising a revenue shall originate in the House of Representatives, but the Senate may propose amendments as in other cases; *provided,* that they shall not, under color of amendment, introduce any new matter, which does not relate to raising a revenue.

Sec. 10. No senator or representative shall, during the term for which he shall have been elected, be appointed to any civil office of profit under this State, which shall have been created, or the emoluments of which increased during such term except such offices as may be filled by elections by the people, *provided, that this prohibition shall not extend to the members of the first Legislature.*

Sec. 11. No member of Congress, nor person holding any office under the United States (post-officers excepted) nor office of profit under this State, justices of the peace, notaries public, coroners and officers of the militia excepted, shall have a seat in either house during his being such member of Congress, or his continuing in such office.

Sec. 12. Neither house shall, during the session, without the consent of the other, adjourn for more than two days, nor to any other place than that in which the houses shall be sitting.

Sec. 13. The Legislature shall, from time to time, provide, as far as practicable, by general laws, for all matters usually appertaining to special or private legislation.

Sec. 14. Corporations shall be formed under general laws, and shall not be created by special acts of the Legislature, except for municipal purposes, and in cases where the objects of the corporation cannot otherwise be attained; and, however formed, they shall forever be subject to the general laws of the State.

Sec. 15. The Legislature shall, by a two-thirds concurrent vote of both branches, have the power to call constitutional conventions, for the purpose of amending this Constitution.

Article V.—Part First

EXECUTIVE POWERS

Sec. 1. The supreme executive power of this State shall be vested in a Governor.

Sec. 2. The Governor shall be elected by the qualified electors, and shall hold his office *one year* from the first Wednesday of January *in each year.*

Sec. 3. The meetings for election of governor shall be notified, held, and regulated, and votes shall be received, sorted, counted, declared and recorded, in the same manner as those for senators and representatives. They shall be sealed and returned into the secretary's office in the same manner, and at the same time as those for senators. And the secretary of state for the time being shall, on the first Wednesday of January, then next, lay the lists before the Senate and House of Representatives, and also the lists of votes of citizens in the military service returned into the secretary's office, to be by them examined, and, in case of a choice by a *majority* of all the votes returned, they shall declare and publish the same. But if no person shall have a *majority* of votes, the House of Representatives shall, by ballot, from the persons having the four highest numbers of votes on the lists, if so many there be, elect two persons and make return of their names to the Senate, of whom the Senate shall, by ballot, elect one, who shall be declared the Governor.

Sec. 4. The Governor shall, at the commencement of his term, be not less than thirty years of age; a natural born citizen of the United States, have been five years, *or from the adoption of this Constitution,* a resident of the State; and at the time of his election and during the term for which he is elected, be a resident of said State.

Sec. 5. No person holding any office or place under the United States, this State, or any other power, shall exercise the office of Governor.

Sec. 6. The Governor shall at stated times, receive for his services a compensation, which shall not be increased or diminished during his continuance in office.

Sec. 7. He shall be commander-in-chief of the army and navy of the State and of the militia, except when called into the actual service of the United States; but he shall not march nor convey any of the citizens out of the State, without their consent or that of the Legislature, unless it shall become necessary, in order to march or transport them from one part of the State to another for the defence thereof.

Sec. 8. He shall nominate, and, with the advice and consent of the council, appoint all judicial officers, coroners, and notaries public; and he shall also nominate, and with the advice and consent of the council, appoint all other civil and military officers, whose appointment is not by this Constitution, or shall not by law be otherwise provided for; and every such nomination shall be made seven days, at least, prior to such appointment.

Sec. 9. He shall from time to time give the Legislature information of the condition of the State, and recommend to their consideration such measures, as he may judge expedient.

Sec. 10. He may require information from any military officer or any officer in the executive department, upon any subject relating to the duties of their respective offices.

Sec. 11. He shall have power, with the advice and consent of the council, to remit, after conviction, all forfeitures and penalties, and to grant reprieves, commutations and pardons, except in cases of impeachment, upon such conditions, and with such restrictions and limitations, as may be deemed proper, subject to such regulations as may be provided by law, relative to the manner of applying for pardons. And he shall communicate to the Legislature at each session thereof, each case of reprieve, remission of penalty, commutation or pardon granted, stating the name of the convict, the crime of which he was convicted, the sentence and its date, the date of the reprieve, remission, commutation or pardon, and the conditions, if any, upon which the same was granted.

Sec. 12. He shall take care that the laws be faithfully executed.

Sec. 13. He may, on extraordinary occasions, convene the Legislature: and in case of disagreement between the two houses with respect to the time of adjournment, adjourn them to such time as he shall think proper, not beyond the day of the next *annual* meeting; and if, since the last adjournment, the place where the Legislature were next to convene shall have become dangerous from an enemy or contagious sickness, may direct the session to be held at some other convenient place within the State.

Sec. 14. Whenever the office of Governor shall become vacant by death, resignation, removal from office or otherwise, the president of the Senate shall exercise the office of Governor until another Governor shall be duly qualified; and in case of the death, resignation, removal from office or disqualification of the president of the Senate, so exercising the office of Governor, the speaker of the House of Representatives shall exercise the office, until a president of the Senate shall have been chosen; and when the office of Governor, president of the Senate, and speaker of the House shall become vacant, in the recess of the Senate, the person, acting as Secretary of State for the time being, shall by proclamation convene the Senate, that a president may be chosen to exercise the office of Governor. And whenever either the president of the Senate or speaker of the House shall so exercise said office, he shall receive only the compensation of Governor, but his duties as president or speaker shall be suspended; and the Senate or House shall fill the vacancy until his duties as Governor shall cease.

ARTICLE V.—PART SECOND

COUNCIL

SEC. 1. There shall be a Council, to consist of seven persons, citizens of the United States, and residents of this State, to advise the Governor in the executive part of government, whom the Governor shall have full power, at his discretion, to assemble; and he with the councillors, or a majority of them, may from time to time, hold and keep a Council, for ordering and directing the affairs of State, according to law.

SEC. 2. The councillors shall be chosen *annually*, on the first Wednesday of January, by joint ballot of the senators and representatives in convention; and vacancies, which shall afterwards happen, shall be filled in the same manner; but not more than one councillor shall be elected from any district, prescribed for the election of senators; and they shall be privileged from arrest in the same manner as senators and representatives.

SEC. 3. The resolutions and advice of Council, shall be recorded in a register, and signed by the members agreeing thereto, which may be called for by either house of the Legislature; and any councillor may enter his dissent to the resolution of the majority.

SEC. 4. No member of Congress, or of the Legislature of this State, nor any person holding any office under the United States, (post officers excepted), nor any civil officers under this State (justices of the peace and notaries public excepted) shall be councillors. And no councillor shall be appointed to any office during the time for which he shall have been elected.

ARTICLE V.—PART THIRD

SECRETARY

SEC. 1. The Secretary of State shall be chosen *annually* at the first session of the Legislature, by joint ballot of the senators and representatives in convention.

SEC. 2. The records of the State shall be kept in the office of the Secretary, who may appoint his deputies, for whose conduct he shall be accountable.

SEC. 3. He shall attend the Governor and Council, Senate and House of Representatives, in person or by his deputies, as they shall respectively require.

SEC. 4. He shall carefully keep and preserve the records of all the official acts and proceedings of the Governor and Council, Senate and House of Representatives, and, when required, lay the same before either branch of the Legislature, and perform such other duties as are enjoined by this Constitution, or shall be required by law.

ARTICLE V.—PART FOURTH

TREASURER

SEC. 1. The Treasurer shall be chosen *annually*, at the first session of the Legislature, by joint ballot of the senators and representatives in convention, but shall not be eligible more than five years successively.

SEC. 2. The Treasurer shall, before entering on the duties of his office, give bond to the State, with sureties, to the satisfaction of the Legislature, for the faithful discharge of his trust.

SEC. 3. The Treasurer shall not, during his continuance in office, engage in any business of trade or commerce, or as a broker, nor as an agent or factor for any merchant or trader.

SEC. 4. No money shall be drawn from the treasury, but by warrant from the Governor and Council, and in consequence of appropriations made by law; and a regular statement and account of the receipts and expenditures of all public money, shall be published at the commencement of the *annual* session of the Legislature.

ARTICLE VI

JUDICIAL POWER

SEC. 1. The judicial power of this State shall be vested in a Supreme Judicial Court, and such other courts as the Legislature shall from time to time establish.

SEC. 2. The justices of the Supreme Judicial Court shall, at stated times receive a compensation, which shall not be diminished during their continuance in office, but they shall receive no other fee or reward.

SEC. 3. They shall be obliged to give their opinion upon important questions of law, and upon solemn occasions, when required by the Governor, Council, Senate, or House of Representatives.

SEC. 4. All judicial officers *now in office or who may be hereafter appointed* shall, *from and after the first day of March in the year eighteen hundred and forty*, hold their offices for the term of seven years from the time of their respective appointments, (unless sooner removed by impeachment or by address of both branches of the Legislature to the Executive) and no longer unless re-appointed thereto.

SEC. 5. Justices of the peace and notaries public, shall hold their offices during seven years, if they so long behave themselves well, at the expiration of which term, they may be re-appointed or others appointed, as the public interest may require.

Sec. 6. The justices of the Supreme Judicial Court shall hold no office under the United States, nor any State, nor any other office under this State, except that of justice of the peace.

Sec. 7. Judges and registers of probate shall be elected by the people of their respective counties, by a plurality of the votes given in at the *annual* election, on the second Monday of September, and shall hold their offices for four years, commencing on the first day of January next after their election. Vacancies occurring in said offices by death, resignation or otherwise, shall be filled by election in manner aforesaid, at the September election next after their occurrence; and in the meantime, the Governor, with the advice and consent of the Council, may fill said vacancies by appointment, and the persons so appointed shall hold their offices until the first day of January *thereafter.*

Sec. 8. Judges of municipal and police courts shall be appointed by the executive power, in the same manner, as other judicial officers, and shall hold their offices for the term of four years; *provided, however, that the present incumbents shall hold their offices for the term for which they were elected.*

Article VII

MILITARY

Sec. 1. The captains and subalterns of the militia shall be elected by the written votes of the members of their respective companies. The field officers of regiments by the written votes of the captains and subalterns of their respective regiments. The brigadier generals in like manner, by the field officers of their respective brigades.

Sec. 2. The Legislature shall, by law, direct the manner of notifying the electors, conducting the elections, and making returns to the Governor of the officers elected; and, if the electors shall neglect or refuse to make such elections, after being duly notified according to law, the Governor shall appoint suitable persons to fill such offices.

Sec. 3. The major generals shall be elected by the Senate and House of Representatives, each having a negative on the other. The adjutant general and quartermaster general shall be chosen *annually* by joint ballot of the senators and representatives in convention. But the adjutant general shall perform the duties of quartermaster general, until otherwise directed by law. The major generals and brigadier generals, and the commanding officers of regiments and battalions, shall appoint their respective staff officers; and all military officers shall be commissioned by the Governor.

Sec. 4. The militia, as divided into divisions, brigades, regiments, battalions and companies pursuant to the laws now in force, shall remain so organized, until the same shall be altered by the Legislature.

Sec. 5. Persons of the denominations of Quakers and Shakers, justices of the Supreme Judicial Court and ministers of the gospel may be exempted from military duty, but no other person of the age of eighteen and under the age of forty-five years, excepting officers of the militia who have been honorably discharged, shall be so exempted, unless he shall pay an equivalent to be fixed by law.

Article VIII

LITERATURE

A general diffusion of the advantages of education being essential to the preservation of the rights and liberties of the people; to promote this important object, the Legislature are authorized, and it shall be their duty to require, the several towns to make suitable provision, at their own expense, for the support and maintenance of public schools; and it shall further be their duty to encourage and suitably endow, from time to time, as the circumstances of the people may authorize, all academies, colleges and seminaries of learning within the State; provided, that no donation, grant or endowment shall at any time be made by the Legislature to any literary institution now established, or which may hereafter be established, unless, at the time of making such endowment, the Legislature of the State shall have the right to grant any further powers to alter, limit or restrain any of the powers vested in, any such literary institution, as shall be judged necessary to promote the best interests thereof.

Article IX

GENERAL PROVISIONS

SEC: 1. Every person elected or appointed to either of the places or offices provided in this Constitution, and every person elected, appointed, or commissioned to any judicial, executive, military or other office under this State, shall, before he enter on the discharge of the duties of his place or office, take and subscribe the following oath or affirmation: " I ——— do swear, that I will support the Constitution of the United States, and of this State, so long as I shall continue a citizen thereof.   So help me God."

" I ——— do swear, that I will faithfully discharge, to the best of my abilities, the duties incumbent on me as ——— according to the Constitution and laws of the State. So help me God." Provided, that an affirmation in the above forms may be substituted, when the person shall be conscientiously scrupulous of taking and subscribing an oath.

The oaths or affirmations shall be taken and subscribed by the Governor and councillors before the presiding officer of the Senate, in the presence of both houses of the Legislature, and by the senators and representatives before the Governor and Council, and by the residue of said officers, before such persons as shall be prescribed by the Legislature; and whenever the Governor or any councillor shall not be able to attend during the session of the Legislature to take and subscribe said oaths or affirmations, said oaths or affirmations may be taken and subscribed in the recess of the Legislature before any justice of the Supreme Judicial Court; *provided, that the senators and representatives, first elected under this Constitution shall take and subscribe such oaths or affirmations before the president of the convention.*

SEC. 2. No person holding the office of justice of the Supreme Judicial Court, or of any inferior court, attorney general, county attorney, treasurer of the State, adjutant general, judge of probate, register of probate, register of deeds, sheriffs or their deputies, clerks of the judicial courts, shall be a member of the Legislature; and any person holding either of the foregoing offices, elected to, and accepting a seat in the Congress of the United States, shall thereby vacate said office; and no person shall be capable of holding or exercising at the same time within this State, more than one of the offices before mentioned.

SEC. 3. All commissions shall be in the name of the State, signed by the Governor, attested by the secretary or his deputy, and have the seal of the State thereto affixed.

SEC. 4. And in case the elections required by this Constitution on the first Wednesday of January *annually*, by the two houses of the Legislature, shall not be completed on that day, the same may be adjourned from day to day, until completed, in the following order; the vacancies in the Senate shall first be filled; the Governor shall then be elected, if there be no choice by the people; and afterwards the two houses shall elect the Council.

SEC. 5. Every person holding any civil office under this State, may be removed by impeachment, for misdemeanor in office; and every person holding any office, may be removed by the Governor, with the advice of the Council, on the address of both branches of the Legislature. But before such address shall pass either house, the causes of removal shall be stated and entered on the journal of the house in which it originated, and a copy thereof served on the person in office, that he may be admitted to a hearing in his defence.

SEC. 6. The tenure of all offices, which are not or shall not be otherwise provided for, shall be during the pleasure of the Governor and Council.

SEC. 7. While the public expenses shall be assessed on polls and estates, a general valuation shall be taken at least once in ten years.

SEC. 8. All taxes upon real and personal estate, assessed by authority of this State, shall be apportioned and assessed equally, according to the just value thereof.

SEC. 9. The Legislature shall never, in any manner suspend or surrender the power of taxation.

SEC. 10. Sheriffs shall be elected by the people of their respective counties, by a plurality of the votes given in on the second Monday of September, and shall hold their offices for two years from the first day of January next after their election. Vacancies shall be filled in the same manner as is provided in the case of judges and registers of probate.

SEC. 11. The attorney general shall be chosen *annually* by joint ballot of the senators and representatives in the convention. Vacancy in said office, occurring when the Legislature is not in session, may be filled by the appointment of the Governor with the advice and consent of the Council.

SEC. 12. But citizens of this State, absent therefrom in the military service of the United States or of this State, and not in the regular army of the United States, being otherwise qualified electors, shall be allowed to vote for judges and registers of probate, sheriffs, and all other county officers *on the Tuesday next after the first Monday in November, in the year one thousand eight hundred and sixty-four, and their votes shall be counted and allowed in the same manner and with the same effect as if given on the second Monday of September in that year. And they shall be allowed to vote for all such officers* on the second Monday in September *annually thereafter forever.* And the votes shall be given at the same time and in the same manner, and the names of the several candidates shall be printed or written on the same ballots with those for Governor, senators and representatives, as provided in section four. article second of this Constitution.

SEC. 13. The Legislature may enact laws excluding from the right of suffrage, for a term not exceeding ten years, all persons convicted of bribery at any election, or of voting at any election, under the influence of a bribe.

SEC. 14. The credit of the State shall not be directly or indirectly loaned in any case. The Legislature shall not create any debt or debts, liability or liabilities, on behalf of the State, which shall singly or in the aggregate, with previous debts and liabilities hereafter incurred at any one time, exceed three hundred thousand dollars, except to suppress insurrection, to repel invasion. or for purposes of war; but this amendment shall not be construed to refer to any money that has been, or may be deposited with this State by the government of the United States, or to any fund which the State shall hold in trust for any Indian tribe.

SEC. 15. *The State is authorized to issue bonds payable within twenty-one years, at a rate of interest not exceeding six per cent. a year, payable semi-annually, which bonds or their proceeds shall be devoted solely towards the reimbursement of the expenditures incurred by the cities, towns and plantations of the State for war purposes during the rebellion, upon the following basis: Each city, town and plantation shall receive from the State one hundred dollars for every man furnished for the military service of the United States under and after the call of July second, eighteen hundred and sixty-two, and accepted by the United States towards its quota for the term of three years, and in the same proportion for every man so furnished and accepted for any shorter period; and the same shall be in full payment for any claim upon the State on account of its war debts by any such municipality. A commission appointed by the Governor and Council shall determine the amount to which each city, town and plantation is entitled; to be devoted to such reimbursement. the surplus, if any, to be appropriated to the soldiers who enlisted or were drafted and went at any time during the war, or if deceased, to their legal representatives. The issue of bonds hereby authorized shall not exceed in the aggregate three million five hundred thousand dollars. and this amendment shall not be construed to permit the credit of the State to be directly or indirectly loaned in any other case or for any other purpose.*

SEC. 16. The Legislature may by law authorize the dividing of towns having not less than four thousand inhabitants. or having voters residing on any island within the limits thereof. into voting districts for the election of representatives to the Legislature, and prescribe the manner in which the votes shall be received, counted. and the result of the election declared.

Article X

SCHEDULE

Sec. 1. All laws now in force in this State, and not repugnant to this Constitution, shall remain, and be in force, until altered or repealed by the Legislature, or shall expire by their own limitation.

Sec. 2. The Legislature, whenever two-thirds of both houses shall deem it necessary, may propose amendments to this Constitution; and when any amendments shall be so agreed upon, a resolution shall be passed and sent to the selectmen of the several towns, and the assessors of the several plantations, empowering and directing them to notify the inhabitants of their respective towns and plantations, in the manner prescribed by law, at their next *annual* meetings in the month of September, to give in their votes on the question, whether such amendment shall be made; and if it shall appear that a majority of the inhabitants voting on the question are in favor of such amendment, it shall become a part of this Constitution.

Sec. 3. *After the amendments proposed herewith shall have been submitted to popular vote, the chief justice of the Supreme Judicial Court shall arrange the Constitution, as amended, under appropriate titles, and in proper articles, parts and sections, omitting all sections, clauses and words not in force, and making no other changes in the provisions or language thereof, and shall submit the same to the Legislature at its next session.* And the draft, and arrangement, when approved by the Legislature, shall be enrolled on parchment and deposited in the office of the Secretary of State; and printed copies thereof shall be prefixed to the books containing the laws of the State. And the Constitution, with the amendments made thereto, in accordance with the provisions thereof, shall be the supreme law of the State.

Sec. 4. Sections one, two and five, of article ten of the existing Constitution, shall hereafter be omitted in any printed copies thereof prefixed to the laws of the State; but this shall not impair the validity of acts under those sections; and section five shall remain in full force, as part of the Constitution, according to the stipulations of said section, with the same effect as if contained in said printed copies.

SELECTED DOCUMENTS

The documents selected for this section have been
chosen to illustrate the various attitudes, concerns
and issues in the development of Maine. Documents relating specifically to the constitutional development
of Maine will be found in volume four of Sources and
Documents of United States Constitutions, a companion
reference collection to the Columbia University volumes
previously cited.

CESSION OF MAINE BY MASSACHUSETTS—1820

An Act in addition to an act entitled "An act relating to the separation of the District of Maine from Massachusetts proper, and forming the same into a separate and independent State."

Be it enacted by the senate and house of representatives of Massachusetts in general court assembled, and by the authority of the same, That the consent of the legislature of this commonwealth be, and the same is hereby, given, that the District of Maine may be formed and erected into a separate and independent State, upon the terms and conditions, and in conformity to the enactments contained in an act entitled "An act relating to the separation of the District of Maine from Massachusetts proper, and forming the same into a separate and independent State," whenever the Congress of the United States shall give its consent thereto, anything in the said act limiting the time when such consent should be given to the contrary notwithstanding: *Provided, however,* That if the Congress of the United States shall not have given its consent, as aforesaid, before the fifteenth day of March next, then all parts of the act, to which this is an addition, and all matters therein contained, which by said act have date or operation from or relation to the fifteenth day of March next, shall have date and operation from and relation to the day on which the Congress of the United States shall give its consent, as aforesaid: *Provided, also,* That if the Congress of the United States shall not give its consent, as aforesaid, within two years from the fourth day of March next, this present act shall be void and of no effect.

SEC. 2. *Be it further enacted,* That if it shall not be known on the first Monday of April next that the Congress of the United States has given its consent, as aforesaid, the people of the said District of Maine shall elect, provisionally, a governor, senators and representatives, or other officers necessary to the organization of the government thereof as a separate and independent State, according to the provisions of the constitution of government agreed to by the people of the said District. And the persons so elected shall assemble at the time and place designated by the said constitution, if the consent of Congress, as aforesaid, shall be given during the present session thereof, but not otherwise; and when assembled, as aforesaid, and having first determined on the returns and qualifications of the persons elected, they shall have the power as delegates of the people for that purpose, to declare, on behalf and in the name of the people, the said elections of such persons to be constitutional and valid, for the respective offices and stations for which they shall have been elected, as aforesaid. And if such declaration shall not be made before the persons so elected shall proceed to transact business as the legislature of said State, the said election shall be wholly void, unless it shall appear that the consent of Congress, aforesaid, shall have been given on or before the said first Monday of April next. And if the consent of Congress, as aforesaid, shall be given after the said first Monday of April next, and the persons so elected, when assembled, as aforesaid, shall not declare the said election valid and constitutional, as aforesaid, within ten days from the last Wednesday of May next, then they shall cease to have any power to act in any capacity for the people of the said District, by virtue of their elections, as aforesaid; and the people shall again choose delegates to meet in convention, in the manner, for the purposes, and with the powers set forth in the third and fourth sections of the act to which this is in addition; the said elections of such delegates to be made on the first Monday of July next, and the delegates to meet in convention at Portland on the first Monday of September next.

[Approved by the governor, February 25, 1820.]

ACT ADMITTING MAINE INTO THE UNION—1820

[Sixteenth Congress. First Session]

Whereas by an act of the State of Massachusetts, passed on the nineteenth day of June, in the year one thousand eight hundred and nineteen, entitled "An act relating to the separation of the District of Maine from Massachusetts proper, and forming the same into a separate and independent State," the people of that part of Massachusetts heretofore known as the District of Maine did, with the consent of the legislature of the said State of Massachusetts, form themselves into an independent State, and did establish a constitution for the government of the same, agreeably to the provisions of the said act: Therefore,

Be it enacted by the Senate and House of Representatives of the United States of America in Congress assembled, That from and after the fifteenth day of March, one thousand eight hundred and twenty, the State of Maine is hereby declared to be one of the United States of America, and admitted into the Union on an equal footing with the original States, in all respects whatever.

Approved, March 3, 1820.

THE STATE OF MAINE

Edward Everett Hale discusses the history of Maine
and describes her natural beauty and traditions.

Outlook, May 6, 1905.

TARRY AT HOME TRAVELS

BY EDWARD EVERETT HALE

*" My mind impels me to write on places where I have been
and on some of the people whom I have seen in them "*

FIRST PAPER

New England—The State of Maine

First of Maine. " Dirigo, I lead," is the fine motto of that State. Its people have no reason to be ashamed of it or to blush because their fathers chose it. It means, if you are modest, that Maine begins the list of the United States, because in those days men began at the north and repeated the list from north to south. So it was Maine, New Hampshire, Vermont. In these days the Pacific State of Washington runs farther north, to the parallel of 49. But in the days of the District of Maine no State ran so near the North Pole as she did. So Maine does lead for every school-boy and every school-girl of America.

If, again, anybody cares, one of Samuel Hale's grandsons moved out into eastern Maine, while one of his sons moved into Connecticut. The son of this Connecticut man was my grandfather. And he was cousin, if you please, of the grandfather of those men from Maine who now find their companions in Senates and stand unawed before kings. But I did not know that when I first went there. I believe I only mention it now to say that the Hales of Maine are our sort of Hales; the Hales of New Hampshire are of the sort of the distinguished lady I have spoken of, and are also of our kind of Hales, "the Hales who do not have sugar in their coffee." The Hales of Vermont are of the Newbury Hales, which means Thomas the Glover. They also are admirable people, and they have a Nathan Hale of their own who was a Captain Nathan Hale of the Revolution, and died on a prison ship in New York harbor and shall be spoken of hereafter. My son Philip is an artist. He was in a New York gallery one day when it was what the artists call " varnishing day," and a lady, referring to his picture, said, " So you have come to New York to be hanged, Mr. Hale." " Yes," said he; " that is the way the Hales usually come."

Perhaps it is as well to say that the Massachusetts Hales are some of them of one kind and some of another, and yet a third belong to the Rehoboth Hales. The Rhode Island Hales are mostly Rehoboth Hales. Besides the Coventry Hales in Connecticut, of whom I am, and the Ashford Hales, who are

our cousins, are the Glastonbury Hales.
They are the people who now produce
peaches for the world, and are our
cousins on another line from the Ashford
Hales.

It is my belief that in all these lines
the Hales were cousins of each other.
Generally speaking, they are tall, with a
tendency to black hair. Without exception they love their country and tell the
truth. So much for genealogy, to which
I may never refer, perhaps, again.

No, I did not go to Maine to see my
cousins. I went there on my way to
New Hampshire to see, if you please, on
those mountains the geographical order
of its stratification. In the year 1841 I
was appointed as a junior member on
the New Hampshire Geological Survey,
under the eminent Charles Thomas Jackson, who is better known as one of the
discoverers of the properties of ether.
On my way to join this survey I went
down to Portland and made a visit on
my lifelong friend Samuel Longfellow.
He is the Longfellow to whom you
owe some of the best hymns in your
hymn-book ; for instance, he wrote the
hymn for my ordination. He graduated
with me at Cambridge in 1839. And
we of our class used to call the cele-
brated Henry Wadsworth Longfellow
the brother of the " Poet Longfellow,"
meaning that he was brother to our Sam.

This narrative should really begin
with a voyage down Portland Harbor in
a boat piloted by Sam Longfellow and
me. He and I and Channing, who had
asked for my appointment on the New
Hampshire Survey, were intimate in college.

From college days down I liked Channing and Channing liked me. In November, 1838, he proposed that we should
watch from midnight down for the annual
recurrence of the meteoric shower which
is now generally called the shower of
the Leonids. And we did so, eight of
us of the college class of 1839, on the
Delta of those days. What says the
poem of that day ?

> Our Chase and our Channing
> The Northwest are scanning,
> While the cold wind is fanning
> Their faces upturned.
> While our Hurd and our Hale,
> With watching turned pale,

> Are looking toward Yale
> Where all these things burned.
> And Morison and Parker
> Cry out to the marker,
> One yet black and darker
> From zenith above.
> While Adams and Longfellow,
> Watching the throng below,
> Won't all night long allow
> Black meteors move.

All the rest of us insisted that there
were black meteors as well as white
ones. This opinion has been confirmed
since then. Our observatory was a
square table, just where the statue of John
Harvard sits in bronze to-day. North,
south, east, and west of the table were
four chairs, facing in those directions, and
in them sat four of the club. A fifth,
with a lantern on the table, recorded the
observations. If any one wants to see
them, he can look in Silliman's Journal
of the next January, or in the Bulletins
of the Astronomical Department of the
French Academy of Sciences. That
was my first appearance on that August
record. The little club of observers
called itself the Octagon Club. Chase
afterwards won distinction as a mathe-
matician. Morison was Provost of the
Peabody Library at Baltimore, Adams
distinguished himself as a lawyer before
his early death, Longfellow was the
preacher and hymn-writer, and Parker
and Hurd every man's friends. We
have never printed till now their " Octag-
onal Scribblings."

And so in 1841 Channing came into
my school-room one day and asked me
to join him as a subaltern in the Geological Survey of New Hampshire, under
Jackson. And, as I have said above, so
I did. If this series ever passes Maine,
and the reader and I should get into
New Hampshire together, I will tell of
those experiences. But now, as I have
said, Maine is the first on the list, and
with Maine we will begin.

To start on this expedition I went to
Portland. Then with Longfellow I
crossed the southwest corner of Maine,
that I might join Channing. In the
expedition which followed we ascended
Mount Washington, as this reader shall
hear when we come to New Hampshire.
So, naturally enough, four years after, he
proposed to me that we should try the

highest mountain in Maine and ascend Mount Katahdin. Before the reader is twenty years older the ascent of Katahdin and the exploration of the Maine lakes will be among the most interesting incidents of familiar summer travel.

But of Maine I knew nothing but the Sebago Lake and the Fryeburg road till I went there with this same William Francis Channing for this Katahdin expedition, as my father had gone to New Hampshire to ascend Mount Washington.

I am writing soon after Channing's death, and I am tempted to say that while he is remembered as a distinguished man of science, it is a wonder to some of us that he never became one of the most distinguished men of his time. He was what is now called a physicist of remarkable resources. He had studied with Dr. Robert Hare, who is still remembered among the fathers of science in America, the inventor of the oxyhydrogen blow-pipe. Channing had early taken up the business of harnessing electricity. He is the author of the fire alarm, now in use in all our cities,

A wizard of such wondrous fame,
    That when in Salamanca's cave
    It listed him his wand to wave,
The bells would ring in Notre Dame.

Indeed, in many lines his early experiments in electricity led the way for those who have given to us the electrical inventions of to-day. I count it as a great misfortune for him that as a little boy he was taken to Europe to school. But Fellenberg was a great apostle of education then; his school at Hofwyl, now forgotten, was the Mecca of educators. For those were the days when even sensible people really thought that people could be instructed into the kingdom of heaven, or practically that if you knew your multiplication table well enough, all else would follow.

Poor little Will Channing, in those early experiences at Hofwyl, lost in childhood the joy and delight, so necessary to the children of God, of easy intercourse with his fellow-men. There was always a certain aloofness about him which made him unhappy. It is not nice to be on the outside margin of any circle of mankind. Here is, for

better, for worse, my explanation of the reason why his name does not stand higher than it does among the men of his generation.

I think he and I were the first persons who had ascended Mount Katahdin with scientific tastes and for any scientific purpose. My dear friend Professor Asa Gray had told me that it was desirable to have specimens of the Alpine vegetation there, that it might be compared with that of Mount Washington. I was able to send him more than twenty varieties on my return.

We consulted with Dr. Jackson, who had been our old chief in New Hampshire, and Dr. Jackson had said, in his offhand way, that, passing across Maine from the coal of Nova Scotia and the limestone of Thomaston, we should come to primitive rock in Mount Katahdin, and that the eastern half of the State of Maine thus presented in very short distances specimens of all the stratifications of the earth's surface from the oldest time to our own. The remark has not much scientific interest, but I have always treasured it as a very good aid to memory as to what Maine is. You can see the beaver build his hut at the north end of Maine; and the next day you can see the Fine Arts Department of Bowdoin College, which is as good a type of the best modern life as you could choose. So you can pass from primitive rock to the latest Tertiary.

Dr. W. O. Crosby, who knows much more about the matter than Dr. Jackson ever pretended to know, says to me, "Between Nova Scotia or Thomaston and Mount Katahdin we have formations covering a wide range of geological time and including some of the oldest as well as the very newest."

If any one is curious about Katahdin, I refer him to the magazine "Appalachia" of April, 1901, where I have printed my journal of the time of that ascent. I have said thus much of it by way of inducing readers to make this excursion.

Very simply, the heart of Maine is "the Lake Country" of the eastern United States, precisely as Minnesota is "the Lake Country" of the Mississippi

Valley, and as we talk of the Lake Country of England when we go to Windermere. No man knows New England as seen by his own eye who has not sat on the higher summits of Katahdin. In Thoreau's books there will be found an account of his ascent. And, not to occupy more space here, I like to say that the adventure which shall take any man up the Kennebec by such of its head waters as come from the north, so that he thus may strike the route of Arnold's detachment of 1775, is a very interesting journey. When Mr. Sparks made that journey in his varied historical research, they told him that no traveler had gone through that way since Arnold's men passed by. Or if you will go up to Houlton, which was a military post in the early part of the last century, you will now find a beautiful modern city with the best appliances. Indeed, Aroostook County, of which Houlton is the shire town, is so prosperous a region that they told me when I was last there that there was not an empty house in the county. I know I found schools with the very latest advantages both in Houlton and Fort Fairfield. And yet, as I said just now, beavers are building their dams in the wilderness there.

The Webster-Ashburton Treaty for the year 1842 settled the old boundary controversy between this country and England, which had existed for nearly sixty years. Mr. Webster and Lord Ashburton were the negotiators, but as the territory in question belonged wholly to the States of Maine and Massachusetts, Mr. Webster had present at Washington four commissioners from Maine, three from Massachusetts, and also my father, Nathan Hale, as his personal friend, because my father had given special attention to the boundary question. There were thus ten persons in all who discussed the subject together. When it was all over, Lord Ashburton told my father that of the ten, he, the English delegate, was the only one who had ever been in the disputed territory. When he was Mr. Baring, he crossed it on a journey between Quebec and Halifax. The route of the New Brunswick and Canada Railway now passes from the southeast to the northwest through the territory which we conceded to England. Half fashionable America knows now how interesting is the region where New England was first settled by the French in 1602. For there is no better central point from which to explore that region than is the town of Bar Harbor. Eastport has some curious history relating to the long period when it was under English government in the War of 1812. It is the only proper American city which has ever been for a long time in the military possession of a foreign power.

But this paper is not written as if it were a guide-book. It is rather as if I met you, Gentle Reader, in a palace car as you and Mrs. Reader and the nine children were speeding eastward from the heats of Baltimore and Philadelphia, and had made up your mind to go as far as you could under the Stars and Stripes. I hope I should not lay out a route for you. I am trying to tell you what are your opportunities in a State which in the continent of Europe would make a very decent empire. Forests and game? Oh, yes. Take the " Flyer " which the Aroostook Railroad people give you, and you will suppose that man was made for nothing but to shoot deer or moose in the wilderness. Or here is another " Flyer " which will tell you about matchless salmon and salmon trout and the rest of the fishy literature. What I want you to understand about Maine is that these people are well poised, well educated, proud, and well satisfied with the place where they are.

It was my duty once to appoint the chief of a new industrial school. Almost of course, I consulted Samuel Armstrong, " the first citizen of America," who was at the head of the Hampton Institute. He said at once, " Go to Maine, and you are almost sure to find the man you want there." He specified their State College at Orono, but he went farther to say that in Maine they had the pure nobility of New England blood, with the simple habits of the old New Englander and the New Englander's determination to excel the rest of mankind. President Robbins, of the Waltham Watch Company, once told me that once a year he sent an accomplished lady into the upper valley of the Kennebec, and that she stayed there a month or two enlisting a party of well-educated young women who should come back with her to Waltham. It is thus, Gentle Reader, that your Waltham watch is one of a company of a million or two, one of which on one happy day once corrected the standard of Greenwich Observatory.

I spoke just now of beavers at the north and of the picture gallery in Bowdoin College which is within smell of the ocean on the south. Do not go up to the north to kill beavers, but you may make yourself a "camp" there and stay a fortnight while you watch their sensible enterprises. Or go down to the Commencement at Bowdoin and find yourself in the midst of their traditions of Hawthorne, Longfellow, Andrew, Chandler, Packard, and Upham, or in that fresh present life which Dr. Hyde leads so well.

I loitered there one day to study the crayons and other drawings which the younger Bowdoin brought from Spain and from Italy. I had never seen that collection rivaled excepting one day when Ruskin showed me somewhat similar portfolios in English Oxford, and I cannot help wishing that somebody, even now, would give us a study of the lives of the two Bowdoins, father and son. Here was the Governor of Massachusetts who, under the name of the " President of the Council," " ran Massachusetts " from 1775 till 1780, and afterwards succeeded Hancock as Governor. Here was his son who was traveling in Europe when Lexington called him home. He was one of our early diplomatists, and he became the benefactor of Bowdoin College. He left his library, his philosophical reports, and his paintings, with six thousand acres of land and the reversion of the island of Naushon, to this College. His mineralogical collection was the nucleus of the cabinets which Professor Cleveland studied and illustrated.

Ah ! here is one of my failures to put the right thread into the right needle at the right time. It must be twenty years ago that I was the guest of the College for some function, and had the pleasure of sitting at the Commencement dinner. Dr. Packard was presiding, loved and honored by everybody who knew him. James Gillespie Blaine was at the height of his fame, and admired and loved by everybody in that assembly. And when he was called upon to speak he spoke with all that personal charm which belonged to his speeches when he was talking of that which really interested him. He characterized Dr. Packard to his face, and, to our delight, told us what manner of man he was. With an old reporter's instinct, I seized the printed menu at my side and began writing on the back the words as they fell from his lips ; but in an instant more some Philistine voice said within me, " Why do you do this ? There are six reporters at their table eagerly taking it better than you could." And I laid my pencil by. Alas and alas ! there was some football match at Princeton or at Harlem that day. The blue pencil of all editorial offices struck out Mr. Blaine's address for the more important details of a touchdown by Smith when Jones had dropped the ball in the gravel, and so that speech was lost. Before the week was over Dr. Packard had died, and I have been left with the wish that on a great occasion I had done what I wanted to do and could do.

MORAL.—It is always better to do a thing than not to do it, if you remember duly the Ten Commandments.

Yes, if there were room to talk of people, there are many, many men who won their laurels in Maine who deserve a place in any Hall of Fame : Champlain, whose monument is his own lake ; Baron Castine, whose life is a romance ; Knox, who "created all the stores of war " and has left behind him men and women for whom we are all grateful (he went down to Maine and opened up Knox County after his last shotted cannon had been fired at Yorktown) ; Lincoln, Washington's friend and sometimes his adviser ; or, in these later days, Evans, Fessenden, James G. Blaine, and my own chief, the President to-day of the United States Senate. How one would like to show how near these men and other Maine men have been to the centers of our American life ! Bowdoin College in her list of alumni counts Hawthorne, Henry Longfellow, Dr. Cleveland, both

Hamlins and Packard and the Chandlers, Carroll Everett, and so many more. Let me for my private pleasure speak of the Greenleafs of Huguenot blood, who came from Newburyport after the war and settled on the upper Penobscot. Of them is Simon Greenleaf, the jurist, and Samuel Greenleaf, who made the map of Maine on the wall yonder. His son was my dear and near friend, my other self, may I say?—Frederic William Greenleaf, who died in 1852. I was thirty, and he a year or two older. He is the Harry Wadsworth of my book "Ten Times One is Ten."

I spoke above of my first visit in Portland. The house on the Main Street is preserved, one is so glad to say in this age of destruction. When I was first there, Judge Longfellow was still alive. He had served the State to great purpose; perhaps he did not know then how his name was going down to the next century. My Samuel Longfellow must have been born in 1819. I saw him first on an August morning in 1835, at about six o'clock in the morning. I had ridden to Cambridge from Boston in what Dr. Holmes would have called a "one-horse chaise," to be examined for admittance at the College. Almost at the moment when we arrived, my brother and I, in front of the University, two more chaises arrived, both of them, as it proved, from the "State of Maine," so simple were the arrangements of those days. In one of them was Francis Brown Hayes, my friend from that hour till he died. In the other was Samuel Longfellow, of whom I may say the same. He was my groomsman when I was married; he wrote the hymn for my ordination. North and south, east and west, we always corresponded with each other. He was one of those, as I have said, who sat where John Harvard now sits counting the shooting stars. And to him you owe some of the best hymns of your happier Sundays. It was he and I who took that voyage of which I have spoken when we counted the islands in Casco Bay. It is queer that I should say this of myself, but it was almost the first time I had ever been in a boat, though I was nineteen years old. From that time till his death he went on, loyal

and brave, without spot or blemish or any such thing, loving and loved. He had seen the vision and he walked with God. He came perfectly naturally into our calling of the ministry. Wherever he was he made a circle of youngsters who loved him and perhaps worshiped him, and lifted them into the Higher Life.

When I made that visit, his charming sisters were in the home. One of them, who left us not long ago, married into the Greenleaf family.

I think Henry Longfellow was there at the same time. I have tried to express in public once and again the blessing which he brought to Harvard College. I mark its history with a line for the day when he came there, only twenty-nine years old. Since that day teacher and pupil, professor and undergraduate, have been of one heart and one soul. Up till that time the etiquette required that a professor should not recognize the existence of a pupil in the college yard. Since that time it has been *we* who are going to do this, *we* who have done that, freshman and dean are all one in the "honorable company of letters." For here was this young fellow, Henry Longfellow, who was not only to teach us but to quicken us and inspire us and make us glad that we were admitted into the secrets of learning and literature. He would walk with us when we took our constitutional, he would play a game of whist with us if we met together at Mrs. Eliot's. He changed the routine of his part of the college from the routine of the class-room to the courtesies and cordialities of a parlor.

And it would take a volume to record what Longfellow was in the amenities and charities of home life. Till he died that old Washington house of his was, one might say, the trysting-place of every tramp from France, or Spain, or Bohemia, or Mesopotamia, or the parts of Libya around Cyrene, who could not speak the English language, and who wanted bread for his mouth and clothes for his back. And not one of these beggars was ever turned away. I believe I never knew but one nobleman of sixteen quarterings. After the days when exiles could return home, he died in his castle on the Danube where his grandfather's grandfather had been born. This man was introduced to me by Henry Longfellow, whom he knew because he had gone to him starving and half naked, in need of everything, and with no claim upon Longfellow but that he had suffered with Kossuth in his country's cause.

They tell me that there are more English men and English women who read and know Longfellow's verses than there are who read and know Tennyson's in the same island. I do not know if this is so. But I can see that it might be so. It is a great thing to be the poet of the People. Do you remember how Dr. Holmes reminded us that Isaac Watts is quoted twenty times every day for once when a line of Pope or Dryden is repeated?

But we are to look in at the windows of other places, upon the faces of other people, and for the moment we must bid good-by to the State of Maine.

WHAT'S THE MATTER WITH MAINE?

This article discusses the economic, political and social issues of the state, indicating the underutilization of natural resources, problems concerning the lumber industry, education, land use, political developments and labor. A detailed analysis of the proposed state constitutional amendment for initiative and referendum is included.

New England Magazine, July, 1907.

WHAT'S THE MATTER WITH NEW ENGLAND?

MAINE: A STUDY IN LAND-GRABBING, TAX-DODGING, AND ISOLATION

By FRANK PUTNAM

WHEN I had completed, in four articles, my pleasant task of introducing Texas to the readers of the NEW ENGLAND MAGAZINE, the Chief said to me:

"Take six months and find out what's the matter with New England. Spend a month in each State, beginning with Maine, and study conditions that make for or against growth and prosperity."

During a month in Maine I observed these facts, explaining why Maine, with natural resources surpassed by those of few American States, has remained almost stationary in population for half a century:

1. Her water-power, amounting to six million units annually, is not used to more than one-twentieth of its extent.

2. The vast forests in Maine's hundreds of unorganized and practically unpopulated townships, over nine million acres in area, are owned by approximately six hundred individuals, firms, and corporations, and pay practically no taxes to the State—three

mills, on a very low valuation, or a fraction over $90,000 a year on a real value variously estimated at from $150,000,000 to $300,000,000.

3. Maine farmers are behind the times — not so much in working their land as in marketing their products. Through lack of organization they get too little for their apples and potatoes, and middlemen get too much.

4. Maine's railways and big manufacturing industries, uniting with the wild-land owners to control the State government, pay low taxes and send most of their surplus earnings out of the State to non-resident owners.

5. Maine's senators and representatives at Washington have constantly advocated and voted for import tariffs that have built up iron and steel mills in other States, but have prevented the use of Canadian iron and coal in creating big steel plants along Maine's unused water-powers. With the substitution of steel for wood in ships, Maine's once great industry of ship-building has been transferred in large part to

other States closer to the American coal and iron deposits. I do not say that if Maine had been able to get duty-free iron and coal from the Canadian provinces she would have set up steel-mills along her unused water-courses, but she could have done so, and in the nature of the case probably would have done so.

6. Maine's politicians, in order to cover their own land-grabbing, tax-dodging, tariff¦ wall-building operations, have kept the State befuddled and deluded with the issue of prohibition of the manufacture and sale of alcoholic liquors.

7. Maine's State normal schools, five of them, are training, at her expense, teachers for other States, since the wages paid teachers in the public schools of Maine are so low that the best teachers find more profitable employment elsewhere. One normal-school principal told me he had two hundred graduates teaching in Massachusetts.

8. Bounded on east, north, and northwest by a foreign country, and on the south by the open sea, Maine has, with a curious contrariety of character, shown indifference — almost hostility — to immigration from other countries, a spirit that I have observed in no other State of the American Union.

9. The daily newspapers of Maine, almost without exception, are apparently owned by, or controlled in the interest of, the wild-land owners, the railroads, or the large manufacturers, so that they offer no sharp and constructive criticism of the policies that have for half a century retarded the development of the State's resources.

10. Until recently, thousands of Maine farmers, tempted by the glorious hunting and fishing all around them, have worked their lands carelessly, so that they did not get the best results either in field or market.

Sons and Daughters Leave Her

Some results flowing from the foregoing facts may be summarized thus:

1. Maine has lost from 5,000 to 10,000 of her brightest sons and daughters annually for half a century; they have found in other States opportunities denied to them at home, and have contributed enormously to the advancement of other commonwealths. It is probable that, in proportion to her population, Maine has contributed to American life more men and women of eminent usefulness than any other State.

2. The State, stripped of its enormous wealth of forests through the folly and faithlessness of her public servants, and by them still denied a fair tax return from these lost lands that once belonged to her, is chronically poor — unable to build and maintain a system of good roads, or adequately to support her public schools. Her teachers, as I said above, are paid less than the unlettered laborers in her fields and forests, and I heard with amazement her Senate haggling over a paltry appropriation of $65,000 for the support of the State University of Maine!

3. Thousands of her small children, who ought to be in school, are devitalizing themselves in her woolen and cotton mills, discounting their maturity to make dividends for non-resident capitalists.

4. Her prohibition law, with its consequent system of spying upon private conduct, has created an atmosphere of hypocrisy and distrust, of cynical disregard of law, and has forced the liquor traffic into the lower levels of society, there to eat away, like a cancer, the character of humbler workers. In Portland alone more than a hundred "kitchen-saloons" — humble homes where housewives dispense bad whiskey secretly to all comers — testify that in a harsh climate and a strenuous, ill-rewarded industrial struggle for life a very large part of society will indulge in the doubtful, degrading pleasure of liquor-drinking, law or no law.

Not Fertilized and Enriched by Immigration

The tides of immigration that have flowed across, fertilized, and enriched nearly all the other States of the Union have passed to the southward of Maine. She has made little or no effort to attract new settlers from other countries; few foreigners have come into Maine except from the French settlements of Canada, and most of these have taken employment at low wages in the textile mills. On the other hand, the men who for fifty years have controlled her political destinies have found their largest personal profit in holding her raw lands out of the market, at low values, while they by one means or another got possession of them. One of the freest and ablest journalists in Maine said to me: "The Know Nothing movement took root in fertile soil in this

State when, in 1854, it dictated the election of the governor and made itself one of the important elements in the formation of the local Republican party. I think it is also the reason for the Maine opposition to tariff reform, which the State so greatly needs. I wonder if you do not overestimate the strength of the feeling against immigration. That opposition does not seem nearly so strong to me as the opposition to tariff reduction, the latter having become equivalent to an article of the creed." My friend misses the point: until the tariffs between Canada and the United States are abolished, or greatly lowered, Maine cannot successfully develop her natural resources so as to attract foreign immigration. What she mistakes for a commendable conservatism is, in my judgment, a blend of isolation and insularity. If the stock of the people of Maine were not one of the strongest, sturdiest, on earth, she would to-day be far worse off than she is. If she could, and would, obtain such changes of the national tariff policy as to enable her to utilize her raw wealth, water-power in combination with Canada's raw wealth of coal and iron, Maine must speedily become one of the wealthiest States in the Union. The highest tribute to the quality of Maine folk is the fact that, despite the policies that have stripped her of her public lands, shackled her hands against natural development, and driven scores of thousands of her strongest sons and daughters to other States, she has within her boundaries, at this day, only five distinct, and small, centres of racial degeneration, and there is no evidence that new centres of this kind are developing.

Let us consider some of the above-mentioned conditions more at length and in detail.

The Story the Figures Tell

Maine, when she separated herself from Massachusetts and set up in business on her own account in 1820, had 298,269 inhabitants; in 1830, 399,455; in 1840, 501,793; in 1850, 583,169; in 1860, 628,279 — showing a steady and healthy growth up to half a century ago. Since then the federal census reports show these figures: 1870, 626,915, or 1,364 less than ten years earlier, due to

losses in war and by emigration to other States, then just beginning; in 1880, 648,936, a gain of only 22,021 in ten years that were years of extraordinary progress throughout the whole north; in 1890, 661,086, or an annual gain, between 1880 and 1890, of only 1,215. In 1900 the State's population was 694,466. The gain in the ten years between 1890 and 1900 was more rapid than in earlier periods, and the indications are that this ratio of gain will increase regularly hereafter. I believe that the people of Maine are on their way out of isolation; that they will in the next decade win their freedom from the cramping restraints that have been laid upon them by narrow and selfish politicians.

It is perhaps too late for the State to regain possession of any large part of the magnificent forest domain of which she has been plundered, but she can, and in my opinion she will, as she ought, levy constantly higher taxes upon those plundered lands, until they shall bear their just proportion of the cost of maintaining the State's institutions upon a scale and in a style suited to the character of her people.

How State Lands Were Alienated

I should require, not a month, but a year, and should need to be, not a reporter, but a detective, in order to trace in detail the processes by which the State of Maine, through successive administrations, alienated her forest wealth. Judging the methods by the results, it seems certain that such a revelation would be shadowed throughout by treacherous graft. Whereas, eighty-seven years ago, the State owned forests worth, even in those days, not less than a hundred millions, and worth to-day, after constant cutting over a large part of their extent, from $150,000,000 to $300,000,000, the State now owns practically none of this land, and has nothing tangible to show for it. The lands are of record as the private property of some six hundred individuals, firms, and corporations, all of whom must have got them either from the State direct or from persons who so got them. It is said that to-day most of the lands are in the hands of "innocent purchasers" — a phrase the employment of which sufficiently indicates the way in which many of the first private owners of the lands got title to them. It is beyond dispute that hundreds of thousands of acres of the most valuable of these lands are to-day owned by men who held State offices when they got the lands from the State. Such transfers are precisely on a par with the scandalous transactions of the officers of the great life-insurance companies, when these persons used the funds of the stockholders for their private profit. And because the trust held by these State officers was a public trust, and the property confided to their care was public property, their dereliction was the graver of the two, the more unworthy. Some of these men still hold high offices, the gift of the people of Maine. The Legislature and the State administrative places are filled with their appointees and adherents. What Maine needs worst of all is a Hughes to uncover their rascality and a free independent newspaper press to scourge them out of public life. It is probably too late to put any of them into prison, where some of them unmistakably belong; the statute of limitations very likely protects them against that measure of justice.

I mention no names — not because there is any least doubt about the facts, but because the fault is not so much that of individuals as of the moral standards of their time and of the antiquated, absurd, awkward system of State government that in Maine as elsewhere makes honest and efficient administration of public affairs almost if not quite impossible. I shall elsewhere return to the discussion of this outworn system of State government — the administration of a business corporation by a board of from two hundred to five hundred directors — a system under which no privately owned business on earth could for a single year escape the bankruptcy court.

These wild forests of Maine even to-day, after more than a century of cutting, cover over 14,000 square miles, or nearly one-half the total area of the State.

By averaging the estimates of five men who have cruised through these forests in the service of lumber-operators for periods ranging from five to fifty years, and by study of official reports, I reach the conclusion that the average value of the standing timber on these lands is to-day not less than

$20 per acre. Deducting 2,000,000 acres for lakes and rivers and cleared spaces within the wild-land area,— and that, I am assured by competent authority, is a liberal deduction,— we have a remainder of 7,000,000 acres whose forest growth alone is worth at least $20 per acre, or a total timber valuation of $140,000,000,— to say nothing of the land value.

These lands, including the timber, are to-day valued by the State assessors, for taxation, at $36,423,301, and paid a total State tax, in 1906, of $91,058.25, under a three-mill levy, as against a total valuation of $340,328,772 for the other half of the State, including cities, villages, and incorporated townships with all cultivated farms. The total State tax, got by a uniform three-mill levy upon all city, village, farm, and wild-land properties, was for 1906 a few thousand less than a million dollars. If the wild lands paid an equitable share of the State's taxation, this figure would be nearly doubled, the burden of excessive taxation now laid upon cities and towns for roads, schools, and the wards of the public could be diminished, and the State could provide as it should for those functions which it ought to take off the shoulders of struggling small communities.

Queer Business for a State to Engage In

She could then, also, abandon the dishonest and disreputable practice of chartering foreign corporations of all characters — and no character — to prey upon the investing public of other commonwealths. No less than one hundred and forty-four pages of the report of the State Board of Assessors for 1906 are filled with the names of corporations which have been chartered under the lax corporation law of the State of Maine. I attempted to total the capitalization of these companies by adding the figures up page by page. At the foot of page 23 I gave up the attempt, and struck an average, adding the totals for the twenty-three pages and dividing the result by twenty-three to get an approximate average for the whole 144 pages. By this method it appears that the State of Maine has chartered more than 6,500 corporations, a very large majority of them foreign,— that is, doing business in other States than Maine,— with a total capitalization — on paper — exceeding three billions of dollars. The State of Maine collected taxes — fees — from these corporations, in 1906, amounting to $144,650.

When you reflect that hundreds of these corporations — to state it mildly — are of the sort that exist only to sell stock, and that other hundreds of them obtained charters in Maine, a State distant from their fields of operation, solely in order that their books might not be too closely scrutinized by public officials in the interest of honest investors, you must be strangely constituted if you do not reach the conclusion that this is a very strange business for a rich, sovereign American State to engage in. There is no evidence that any of the State's politicians ever got much money out of this business. The Secretary of State and the attorney-general, for filing and for examining papers, respectively, formerly got a special, personal fee from each such corporation, and in the case of one attorney-general these fees amounted to twenty-odd thousand dollars; but the Legislature has since abolished these personal fees, I am told.

Maine might well have saved her reputation for business sense and business honesty by getting this $144,650 from some other source — by placing something approaching an honest valuation upon the wild lands, for example. It would have been better for her to allow New Jersey to hold a monopoly of this form of financial swindling — better not only for Maine, but for the thousands of honest corporations that in good faith have taken charters under her law, since the general public, in view of this wholesale granting of charters for petty fees to all comers, responsible or otherwise, must soon come to regard a Maine charter as a just cause for suspecting that the corporation holding it has some good reason for not wishing to take a charter from a State that exercises a real guardianship of its investors. If you regard my conclusions as open to doubt, by all means write to the Board of Assessors at Augusta, get a copy of their report, and read through the long list of corporations, capitalized at from a million to twenty millions, whose very names smack of quackery. Many of them you have seen advertised in the mining-stock columns of the daily papers of late — and not a few of them you have seen denounced in the columns of journals that have made efforts to pro-

tect their readers against specious and swindling offers of such stocks.

There is something especially humorous — or otherwise, as you look at it — in this spectacle of a State that is too pure to take a revenue from the sale of liquors, but not too pure to lend its name to a lot of stock-peddling sharps in a hundred different doubtful fields. I hold no brief for liquor-sellers; I have no doubt the world will be far better off than it is when man is sufficiently civilized to avoid the use of alcoholic stimulants. But since he is what he is, and obviously will have the stuff, good or bad, legally or illegally, it may be worth while to note the fact that, whereas Portland spends $75,000 a year for her police force, has more than 2,100 arrests yearly for violations of the liquor law, and gets no revenue from the traffic, Paterson, New Jersey, with about the same population, more than supports her police force from the revenue of the liquor traffic and has less than one-half as many annual arrests for violations of the liquor laws.

The average tax on that half of the State of Maine not owned by the wild-land barons who control the State government is twenty mills. This includes municipal, county, and state taxation. The total taxes paid by the wild-land owners in the unincorporated townships average a fraction under five mills,— three mills to the State and less than two mills for county purposes.

Mr. Dennett's Campaign for Equal Taxation

In 1890, when Mr. Liberty B. Dennett, of Portland, contemporary and peer of Thomas B. Reed and one of the "noblest old Romans" in the State, began his agitation for an increase of taxation on the wild lands the valuation set upon these lands by the assessors was less than $9,000,000, and the State derived a tax revenue from them of less than $30,000. Although Mr. Dennett has conducted this agitation single-handed, practically without aid or comfort from politician or press of any party, he has made a strong impression upon the public mind, and has seen the valuation of the wild lands advanced fourfold in seventeen years.

Indeed, so strongly has Mr. Dennett impressed his propaganda upon the people that the wild-land barons and their political vassals hate him with an unholy hatred, dub him crank and nuisance, and angrily refuse to discuss him or his agitation. When I asked Governor Cobb, a cultivated gentleman, to give me the other side of the story, he retorted impatiently, "If you mean old Dennett's talk, I don't care to say anything about it." I owe it to the Governor to explain that he was at the time engrossed, and not improbably irritated, by the pressure of the closing days of a legislative session in which his pet measure, the Sturgis law, was strongly assailed, both inside and outside of his own party, and his temper was very likely not at its normal gauge. "Old Dennett" is now waging a systematic campaign of education through the pages of *The Pine Tree Magazine* of Portland, and I venture to predict that at no distant date his revelations and arguments will bear fruit in measures equalizing taxation in Maine.

Four years ago Mr. Dennett induced a member from Portland (who, to preserve his standing with the powers that be in his party, gave notice that he personally did not favor the measure) to offer a bill providing for a State levy of fifteen mills upon the wild lands. The committee to which the bill was referred reported that it ought to pass, and the wild-landers were scared stiff. Nothing like this had ever menaced them before. Exerting their control of the situation, they brought the matter before the State Supreme Court for an opinion as to the constitutionality of the proposition. The court unanimously reported that it was unconstitutional. It may have been so; but the fact that four of the eight members of The court were, either personally or through members of their families, interested as proprietors of wild lands left their finding under a grave shadow. Judges concerned for their honor would have declined to sit in the hearing of any question in which they had a personal interest at stake. It speaks volumes for the perfection of the political machine that dominates Maine that none of the four judges interested in the wild lands was visibly troubled by any scruple against sitting in judgment upon a question in which he had a direct pecuniary interest.

The Desired Constitutional Amendment

Mr. Dennett, fronted by this finding of the Supreme Court, framed a petition for a constitutional amendment, as follows:

To the Honorable Senate and House of Representatives in Legislature assembled at Augusta, A.D. 1907: —
Respectfully represent your petitioners, citizens of Maine, that under the constitution of this State as construed by our Supreme Judicial Court, the lands in the unincorporated townships of our State, called "wild lands," cannot be assessed by our Legislature at a greater rate on a dollar upon their valuation than that assessed upon our municipalities. Consequently the less the rate assessed upon our cities and towns, the less the tax rate the owners of the wild lands will have to pay; *and in the event that the income from other sources of taxation should equal all demands upon the state treasury, so that no tax upon our municipalities, by the State, would be necessary, the wild lands would escape all taxation, except a county tax.* Whereas, our towns and cities must ever and forever tax all their properties at a rate many times in excess of taxes heretofore assessed by the State upon wild lands, in order to maintain their roads, their paupers, their schools, and other institutions for which purposes the wild lands are not taxed, notwithstanding owners of wild lands, resident within the State, have equal protection of our laws, and all civic privileges accorded all other citizens; thereby placing them under equal obligation.

Therefore it becomes necessary to amend our State Constitution, otherwise the colossal injustice which all the tax-payers of our towns and cities have suffered in the past must be continued in the future, and we respectfully pray that your honorable Senate and House will pass the necessary resolutions submitting to the voters of the State at our next election the following amendment to Section 8 of Article IX of our Constitution so that it shall read when amended as follows, viz.:

"All taxes on real and personal estate, assessed by authority of this State, shall be apportioned and assessed equally, according to the just value thereof; and lands in the unincorporated townships of the State shall be assessed by the Board of State Assessors at the same rate as the average rate of municipal taxation throughout the State; and the wild lands, so called in the plantations, shall be assessed at said rate, only diminished by deducting the rate of taxation assessed by said plantation upon the property of the plantation. Also from said average rate of municipal taxation shall be deducted the rate of the county tax assessed upon the several counties containing wild lands, so that the wild lands in all the counties containing them shall be assessed and pay a tax to the State at a rate which shall be equal to the average rate of municipal taxation through out the State."

Needless to say, this proposal received scant courtesy in the session of 1907. Under the laws of Maine, the only way in which the Constitution can be amended is through the action of the Legislature in passing, by a two-thirds vote of both houses, a measure for submission to the people at the next biennial election. And needless to say, there is no remote possibility that the Legislature, as at present constituted, will ever pass a measure looking to adequate taxation of the wild lands.

There is a gleam of hope, however — two gleams, to be precise. It was pointed out to me by a member of the State Board of Assessors that the burden of taxes might be more equitably distributed should the State assume the burden of public roads and public education, either wholly or in larger measure than at present. In this case, the cities, villages, and farms would be relieved of all or a part of their local taxes now devoted to roads and schools, and the State, having assumed these burdens, would have to levy a higher rate than three mills in order to get sufficient revenue to meet its new expenses. This method would increase the total levy on wild lands and at the same time lower the total levy on other property.

Maine Moves Toward Direct Legislation

The second gleam of hope — and the brighter one, in my opinion — was the passage, by the Legislature of 1907, of a constitutional amendment to be submitted to the voters in 1908, providing for the initiative and referendum. True, this proposal limits the action of the amendment to statute law, but it is a long first step away from oligarchy toward pure democracy, and is pretty sure to be followed, in due season, by an extension of its operations to include the provisions of the Constitution. With all her boasted conservatism, Maine will probably not long wish to stand in the attitude of a commonwealth that dare not trust the making of organic law in the hands of her citizens. This would be to admit that her standard of citizenship is so low that the law-making power cannot safely be entrusted to the people, but must be safe-guarded in the hands of their representatives. It is to assert that the directors of the corporation, the legislators, are beyond the reach of the stockholders, the people, and entitled of right to wield a power upon which the stockholders can set no check. I doubt if the people of Maine will for long be willing to submit to any such assumptions. State-of-Maine folk are proud and self-reliant, as well as sturdy and long-suffering. They will come into their own finally.

It is a curious fact that most of the committeemen who reported this popular government bill favorably were personally opposed to it; they felt the popular demand for it and dared not oppose it as they wished to do. For this measure, the State has to thank the Referendum League, a little group of enthusiasts commanding neither wealth nor political power, save as they were felt to represent the popular wish. Mr. Kingsbury B. Piper, a legislative newspaper correspondent and the secretary of the League, told me how the measure had been promoted, modestly minimizing his own part in the campaign. The League drew its bill and first tried to obtain the endorsement of Obadiah Gardner, the master of the State Grange. Mr. Gardner did not even reply to the letter the League addressed to him, and in which he was asked to endorse the movement. The League's officers, arguing that after all it would be better to get the endorsement of the Grange through its rank and file, dropped Mr. Gardner from consideration and obtained the passage of resolutions favorable to the initiative and referendum at the next annual session of the State Grange. Mr. Gardner would not assist, but he did not openly oppose the resolutions.

Now the State Grange has lodges in almost every corner of Maine. The farmers and their wives to the number of more than 60,000 take a pride in it; its political influence is therefore not to be despised, not even by a political machine so strongly intrenched as that of the Republican party in Maine. Wherefore, when, having obtained the Grange's endorsement, the Referendum League folks approached the chairmen of the Republican and Democratic State Committees, they were accorded more respectful attention than they had been accustomed to get in those quarters. The Republican chairman consented to endorse the movement as applied to statute law only, and the Republican State Convention next following wrote a referendum-plank of this character into its platform. The Democrats, seeing in the new movement a means whereby they might possibly get the prohibitory amendment resubmitted to the people, endorsed the League's bill without reservations. They wanted the Constitution brought within the workings of the proposed amendment, and said so in their State platform. The Prohibition party was shy for a time, but on being convinced that the League did not aim at the liquor

amendment, and in view of the certainty
that the Republican majority in the Legislature would not pass a referendum bill to
apply to anything more than statute law, the
Prohibitionists also endorsed the League's
work. The Socialist party did so as a matter of course, since it was a movement in
their own general direction, to restore the
government to the people.

With endorsements from all four parties
in State Convention, the Legislature, notwithstanding a large majority of its members were temperamentally as well as log-
ically opposed to direct legislation, did not
dare defeat this bill. It got the necessary
two-thirds majority in each house, and was
signed by the Governor. It was the most
important act of the Legislature of 1907,
and probably the most far-reaching act of
any Maine Legislature during the last fifty
years.

Should the voters of Maine give this proposal a majority in 1908, and there is every
reason to believe that they will, the people
of Maine will thereafter have the power to
make new laws with or without the consent
of Legislature and Governor, and will have
the further power to veto laws made by
Legislature and Governor. In brief, this
is the working of the plan proposed.

Terms of the Proposed Amendment

Part First of Article 4 of the State Constitution is amended to read:

The legislative power shall be vested in two distinct branches, a House of Representatives and a
Senate, each to have a negative on the other, and
both to be styled the Legislature of Maine; but
the people reserve to themselves power to propose laws and to enact the same at the
polls independent of the Legislature, and also reserve power at their own option to approve or reject at the polls any act, bill, resolve, or resolution
passed by the joint action of both branches of the
Legislature, and the style of their laws and acts
shall be, "Be it enacted by the people of the State
of Maine."

Part Third of Article 4 is amended to
read:

The Legislature shall convene on the first
Wednesday of January, biennially, and, with the
exceptions hereinafter stated, shall have full power
to make and establish all reasonable laws and regulations for the defense and benefit of the people
of this State, not repugnant to this Constitution
nor to that of the United States.

Part Third of Article 4 is further
amended by the addition of these sections:

Section 16. No act or joint resolution of the
Legislature, except such orders or resolutions as
pertain solely to facilitating the performance of
the business of the Legislature, of either branch,
or of any committee or officer thereof, or appropriate money therefor, or for the payment of sal-
aries fixed by law, shall take effect until ninety
days after the recess of the Legislature passing it,
unless in case of emergency (which with the facts
constituting the emergency shall be expressed in
the preamble of the act) the Legislature shall, by
a vote of two-thirds of all the members elected to
each house, otherwise direct. An emergency bill
shall include only such measures as are immediately necessary for the preservation of the public
peace, health, or safety; and shall not include (1)
an infringement of the right of home rule for municipalities, (2) a franchise or a license to a corporation or an individual to extend longer than
one year, or (3) provision for the sale or purchase
or renting for more than five years of real estate.

Section 17. Upon written petition of not less
than ten thousand electors, addressed to the Governor and filed in the office of the Secretary of
State within ninety days after the recess of the
Legislature, requesting that one or more acts, bills,
resolves, or resolutions, or part or parts thereof,
passed by the Legislature, but not then in effect
by reason of the provisions of the preceding section, be referred to the people, such acts, bills, resolves, or resolutions, or part or parts thereof, as
are specified in such petition shall not take effect
until thirty days after the Governor shall have announced by public proclamation that the same
have been ratified by a majority of the electors voting thereon at a general or special election. As
soon as it appears that the effect of any act, bill,
resolve, or resolution, or part or parts thereof, has
been suspended by petition in manner aforesaid,
the Governor, by public proclamation, shall give
notice thereof and of the time when such measure
is to be voted on by the people, which shall be at
the next general election not less than sixty days
after such proclamation; or, in case of no general
election, within six months thereafter the Governor
may, and, if so requested in said written petition
therefor, shall order such measure submitted to
the people at a special election not less than four
nor more than six months after his proclamation
thereof.

Section 18. The electors may propose to the
Legislature for its consideration any bill, resolve,
or resolution, including bills to amend or repeal
emergency legislation, but not an amendment of
the State Constitution, by written petition addressed to the Legislature or to either branch
thereof, and filed in the office of the Secretary of
State or presented to either branch of the Legislature at least thirty days before the close of its session. Any measure thus proposed by not less than
twelve thousand electors, unless enacted without
change by the Legislature at the session at which
it is presented shall be submitted to the electors,
together with any amended form, substitute, or
recommendation of the Legislature, and in such
manner that the people can choose between the
competing measures or reject both. When there
are competing bills and neither receives a majority
of the votes given for or against both, the one receiving the most votes shall, at the next general
election, to be held not less than sixty days after
the first vote thereon, be submitted by itself if it re-

ceives more than one-third of the votes given for or against both. If the measure initiated is enacted by the Legislature without change, it shall not go to a referendum vote unless in pursuance of a demand made in accordance with the preceding section. The Legislature may order a special election on any measure that is subject to a vote of the people. The Governor may, and if so requested in the written petition to the Legislature shall, by proclamation, order any measure proposed to the Legislature by at least twelve thousand electors as herein provided, and not enacted by the Legislature without change, referred to the people at a special election to be held not less than four nor more than six months after such proclamation; otherwise said measure shall be voted upon at the next general election held not less than sixty days after the recess of the Legislature to which such measure was proposed.

Section 19. Any measure referred to the people and approved by a majority of the votes given thereon shall, unless a later date is specified in such measure, take effect and become a law in thirty days after the Governor has made public proclamation of the result of the vote on said measure, which he shall do within ten days after the vote thereon has been canvassed and determined. The veto power of the Governor shall not extend to any measure approved by vote of the people, and any measure initiated by the people and passed by the Legislature without change, if vetoed by the Governor and if his veto is sustained by the Legislature, shall be referred to the people to be voted on at the next general election. The Legislature may enact measures expressly conditioned upon the people's ratification by a referendum vote.

Section 20. As used in either of the three preceding sections the words "electors" and "people" mean the electors of the State qualified to vote for Governor; "recess of the Legislature" means the adjournment without day of a session of the Legislature; "general election" means the November election for choice of presidential electors or the September election for choice of Governor and other state and county officers; "measure" means an act, bill, resolve, or resolution proposed by the people, or two or more such, or part or parts of such, as the case may be; "written petition" means one or more petitions written or printed, or partly written and partly printed, with the original signatures of the petitioners attached, verified as to the authenticity of the signatures by the oath of one of the petitioners certified thereon, and accompanied by the certificate of the clerk of the city, town, or plantation in which the petitioners reside, that their names appear on the voting-list of his city, town, or plantation as qualified to vote for Governor. The petitions shall set forth the full text of the measure requested or proposed. The full text of a measure submitted to a vote of the people under the provisions of the Constitution need not be printed on the official ballots, but, until otherwise provided by the Legislature, the Secretary of State shall prepare the ballots in such form as to present the question or questions concisely and intelligibly.

Section 21. The City Council of any city may establish the initiative and referendum for the electors of such city in regard to its municipal affairs, provided that the ordinance establishing and providing the method of exercising such initiative and referendum shall not take effect until ratified by vote of the majority of the electors of said city, voting thereon at a municipal election. Provided, however, that the Legislature may at any time provide a uniform method for the exercise of the initiative and referendum in municipal affairs.

Section 22. Until the Legislature shall enact further regulations not inconsistent with the Constitution for applying the people's veto and direct initiative, the election officers and other officials shall be governed by the provisions of this Constitution and of the general law, supplemented by such reasonable action as may be necessary to render the preceding sections self-executing.

How the Idea Got Root in Maine

Maine's direct legislation campaigners got their inspiration from the far West. Mr. Piper was teaching school in California in 1894, and Oregon's direct legislation scheme struck him as the best means by which to shake loose "Blind Boss" Buckley's grip on San Francisco. He saw the initiative and referendum work out good results in the West, and when he returned to Maine he perceived the need of it there. He supported the Clark resolve, which failed in the Legislature of 1905, and during the session of 1907, being stationed at the capitol as a newspaper correspondent, he saw the Weeks resolve pass both houses without a dissenting vote.

Roland T. Patten, of Skowhegan, editor of *The Somerset Reporter*, is another who did pioneer work for direct legislation in Maine. Mr. Patten's father was a Republican politician, senator from Piscataquis County in 1868 and 369. He had the friendship of Blaine and Hamlin, and the younger Patten recalls the day when these two eminent men dined at the family home in Monson as the red-letter day of his youth. When twenty-six years of age Mr. Patten was elected treasurer of Somerset County, and all things seemed to indicate that he would be content to be a spoke in the wheel, made up of the rings and bosses which were governing his State. About the end of his tenth year as county treasurer, however, he heard of the initiative and referendum. He wrote the following plank and asked that it be made a part of the political platform of his party at the county convention then about to be held:

"We believe in the rule of the majority, and demand that a constitutional amendment, embodying the principles of direct legislation, be

submitted to the people of this State."

The Committee of Resolutions refused to submit the plank to the convention; the party bosses scouted the idea. Mr. Patten refused to accept a renomination and quit the party. This was in 1902. In succeeding years Mr. Patten made it his business to offer planks favoring direct legislation to all conventions, of either party, held in his County, and to the State Conventions of both the Republican and Democratic parties. The Democratic State Convention of 1902 accepted and placed in its platform the plank offered by him, identically as it was written; other than this, his offers invariably met with chilling reception.

The first initiative and referendum resolve ever presented to a Maine Legislature was furnished by Mr. Patten and offered in the House of Representatives by Cyrus W. Davis, of Waterville, in January, 1903. Representative Davis, Senator Forrest Goodwin, of Skowhegan, and Mr. Patten were the only persons to appear at the committee hearing on the measure. It was referred to the succeeding Legislature.

From this time on Mr. Patten commenced to get in touch with others who were at work toward the same end. He had previously been alone, or, if there were others in sympathy with the movement in Maine, he did not know of them. The Referendum League of Maine was organized, and he became the press representative. He had, some years direct legislation, and through them he was able to get material for arguments that were unanswerable. His favorite method was to cut clippings from papers which commented adversely on the principle and send them to his correspondents to be answered. Mr. Patten's favorite saying is, "As to my family, I will enjoy nothing in which they may not share; as a citizen, I will demand only that for which I can secure the approval of the majority."

The State Unmistakably Desires It

Granting that to levy upon wild lands a higher rate of taxation for State purposes than is levied upon other property is unconstitutional, no one pretends that, if submitted to a popular vote of the State such a levy would fail to be ordered. Indeed, it is because the wild-land owners are convinced of the inequitable nature of the present tax that they have so strongly fought at every step against the opening of this question to public consideration. When in 1903 a leg-

islative committee by a vote of five to two reported that the bill proposed by Mr. Dennett ought to pass, Mr. Bass, the publisher of *The Bangor Commercial,* and a wild-land owner, sent out a call to other wild-land owners to raise a fund of $12,250 to fight the bill in the Legislature. In that letter Mr. Bass said, among other things:

"It requires a two-thirds vote of the Legislature to refer to the people an amendment to the State Constitution; *and with the practical certainty that they would vote this measure, should the constitutional amendment be submitted to them,* it is very important that we have such an action as will count in defeating the measure before the Legislature."

Well, the wild-landers got the "action" — through the Supreme Court, one-half of whose members were wild-landers — and got it without forcing the legislators to show their hands by voting for or against a proposition which was "practically certain to be approved by the people" should they get a chance to vote upon it. In plain English, as put by Mr. Dennett in one of his articles, "Our servants, the senators and representatives of the last Legislature, tyranically denied the people their absolute right to decide and determine for themselves whether the Constitution should be so amended that the wild lands may be equally taxed with all the other property of the State."

To-day the State of Maine owns, out of all the magnificent domain that was once its property, a few small and scattered pieces, among them a single tract of some twenty thousand acres of forest lands in Indian township, Aroostook County. For half a century this land had been cut over at intervals by private companies under leases from the State, yet to-day the value of the standing timber upon it, counting only trees above five inches in diameter breast high, is officially stated to be $259,000. How the land-grabbers missed getting title to this township is more than I can learn. Perhaps they left it in the State's hands as a practice-ground for the making of forestry experiments at public expense, and for their own chief ultimate benefit. At any rate, the State still miraculously owns it, and will presumably make it a permanent forest reservation, an adjunct to the Department of Forestry in the State University, and a source of revenue sufficient to cover the cost of maintaining it.

Conservation of the State's Forests

Aside from the problem of equalizing taxation so as to get State revenues large enough to enable the State fitly to fulfil its proper functions, the great problem before the State to-day is the conservation of its forests. The best estimates that I could obtain put the total annual takings of timber from Maine forests at a billion feet. The larger wild-land owners, as the Coe-Pingree Company, holding one and one-half million acres, and the two great paper companies,— the International and the Great Northern,— as well as many smaller holders, are adopting practices calculated to maintain the value of their holdings. The Legislature has put no restrictions upon timber-cutting, but the State Forestry Department, aided by the National Bureau of Forestry, has taught the wisdom of cutting no trees less than ten inches in diameter, breast high. The Legislature appropriates $10,000 annually to maintain a system of forest fire-wardens, and private owners of wild lands have contributed to the support of this service. Aside from reckless cutting, the principal losses to the forests are from fires. Many of these losses result from careless treatment of camp-fires in hunting and fishing camps, and from equally reckless handling of brush-fires lighted by settlers while clearing their lands for agricultural purposes. This explains, in part, the policy of hostility shown by wild-land owners toward the settlement of the wild lands by home-makers. It offers a reason for the State's policy of indifference to immigration. It illuminates that curious hermit tendency noticeable in Maine, as contrasted with the eagerness of other States possessing unused land to win settlers from other countries.

There is a growing fear lest the too rapid destruction of the forests of Northern Maine shall detrimentally affect the flow of the rivers that afford water-power for the manufacturing industries in the southern half of the State. An impression grows that the State cannot safely leave to the discretion of the private owners of the State's great northern forests the entire responsibility for the risk involved in this problem. Moreover, one of the great annual money crops of Maine is her summer visitors. Many of them are attracted to Maine by the hunting and fishing there found on a scale not equalled elsewhere in all the East. One of the stock arguments offered by wild-land owners against paying higher taxes is this: that their lands are treated as a great public game-preserve, to which the State invites hundreds of thousands of visitors annually; that these visitors, hunting over the private property of the wild-landers, leave in the State every year from ten to fifteen million dollars, which is taken by farmers, inn-keepers, and railroads and that these visitors, through their carelessness with fire, cause large losses to the forest holdings of the wild-landers. The wild-land owners say — some of them put it in the form of a threat — that if they are compelled to pay taxes as proposed by Mr. Dennett they could not afford to conduct cutting so as to preserve the forests, but would be forced in self-preservation to make a clean sweep of their woods in order to escape what would amount practically to confiscation. Within bounds, there is truth and justice in these contentions. Let the tax be set so high that a forest-owner cannot afford to cut gradually and take a limited annual income from his property and he will naturally feel impelled to cut enough each year to keep ahead of the tax-gatherers.

But perhaps the people of the State, operating under the new direct-legislation law, would have something more to say at this point, should the wild-land owners assume so to interpret an increased tax rate. Hitherto for half a century the wild-land owners have had their own sweet will in making the laws of the State. Meantime, other interests have become conscious politically. These other interests embrace a vast majority of the electorate. They might reasonably assume the right to determine whether any given increase in the tax levy should justify wild-land owners in slaughtering their forests. The maxim of "the greatest good to the greatest number," though long dormant in Maine, has not been outlawed in consequence, and might conceivably again be invoked to save the rights of the majority in the State's forests, despite the attitude of their private owners.

With the decline of other American woodlands under the axe and saw, the value of the Maine forests constantly rises, and the annual takings of lumber in one form or another is larger each year. Sawmills

and pulp-mills multiply along all the established river routes and railroads, and new
railroad extensions are soon to open up vast
tracts of timber in Northwestern Maine.
In 1908 and 1909 the Bangor & Aroostook
Railroad will build a line from West Seebois
150 miles north and west along the eastern
border of Lake Chesuncook and the Alle-
gash River to St. Francis on the Canadian
border. The Portland & Rumford Falls
Railroad, before its recent absorption by
the Maine Central, had plans for an extension northward from its present terminus
on Moosehead Lake to the Canadian border, west of the new extension of the Bangor
& Aroostook, and for an extension southward to Portland. It proposed also to build
new docks at Portland. It is likely that the
Maine Central will carry out the plan for
extension northward, but unlikely that it
will, at present, construct new docks at Portland. In any event, it seems certain that
unless some close regulation of cutting is
enforced by the State the increased demand
for forest products will result in a rapid
diminution of Maine's forest areas.

Already the caribou is practically extinct
in Maine, and the pine long since lost its
place at the head of the list of Maine's forest assets. "Sixty years ago"— I quote
from the report of the State Forest Commissioner for 1906 —"the pineries of Maine
and lower Canada contained stores of white
pine which were believed to be practically
inexhaustible; but the larger part has already been cut, and the great trees that were
once the pride of the northern forest no
longer exist." "During 1905 there were
100,000,000 feet of second-growth white
pine manufactured in Maine, and the sup-
ply in the southern part of the State appears to be increasing."

The spruce has succeeded the pine as the
chief asset of the Maine forests, and the annual cut of this wood is now above 700,000,-
000 feet, and rapidly increasing. Its supreme adaptability for paper pulp marks it
for destruction unless State laws shall be in-
terposed to save it. The experience of other
States that left the "regulation" of their
forest supplies in private hands affords a
melancholy example of the futility of such
a course. The destruction of the magnificent forests of Michigan and Wisconsin
produced a few multi-millionaire United
States senators and a temporary prosperity

for a limited part of the population of those
States. The forests of Texas, now chiefly in
the hands of huge corporations mainly financed by Northern capitalists, are being
slaughtered, and that State will in due time
join the list of commonwealths that have
regrets in place of their once splendid woodlands.

Comical Railroad Tax Rebates

I have said that the railroads and wild-
land owners work together to control the
State government in Maine. As Mr. Dennett puts it, the wild-land moose and the
railroad-tiger hunt together in the jungle of
Maine politics. You have seen what the
wild-landers got out of the partnership.
The railroads got large land grants, some
of them, and others had to be content with
contracts with the State whereunder they
escaped paying the bulk of taxes that would
otherwise have been laid upon them, in consideration of agreeing to carry the troops of
the State free of charge during the next war.
It would seem as if some humorist must
have suggested the terms of those contracts;
yet a sober gentleman at the State-house explained to me that the State took this means
of giving subsidies to railroad builders, being
forbidden or not empowered by the Constitution to give subsidies directly. Doubt-
less the development that has followed the
construction of the roads has amply recom-
pensed the State for its quaint tax exemp-
tions. The public sentiment adverse to
this form of subsidy has, however, crystal-
lized in a resolution of the Legislature of
1907 not to make such contracts in future.
Those now in force have limited terms to
run, and will be honored until they expire.

The total taxes levied on the 2,093 miles
of railroads in Maine in 1906 were $494,-
118.92. Of this amount, $56,760.76 was re-
bated, under the contracts covering the free
carriage of the State's troops "during the
next war." Of this rebate the Bangor &
Aroostook got $51,277.96. The total State
tax levied on the 482 miles of this road was
$53,976.80. Add to this the share of the
cost of the State Railroad Commission apportioned to the Bangor & Aroostook, and
its total payments to the State for 1906, net,
were $4,402.43. The Bangor & Aroostook,
on a capitalization of about $30,000 a mile,

pays four per cent dividends and has a comfortable annual surplus. It is this year building a cut-off, to shorten its main line northward, at a cost of a million, and is also double-tracking a part of its line, in order to handle the freight business. It has made a new harbor at Stockton Springs, at the mouth of the Penobscot River, equal, if not superior, to the harbor at Portland, and has built there enormous docks and warehouses to handle its huge traffic in potatoes and lumber. This road also has in hand, for 1907 and 1908, a project for the construction of 150 miles of new road up through the northwestern part of the State. It is a live factor in the new prosperity of Maine, was planned and to a large extent financed by Maine men, and, if it is ever right for the State to go into partnership with private undertakings, this is one of those which justify the proceeding; for the Bangor & Aroostook has done more to advance the prosperity of Maine during the last dozen years than any other single factor. The Somerset and Washington County railroads are now part of the Maine Central, otherwise the Boston & Maine system, and the total of their rebates, $5,482.60, goes to fatten the treasury of that very prosperous corporation. The rebates were not voted to the Maine Central direct, but became one of its perquisites when, the small independent roads having become bankrupt, they were assimilated by the larger company.

I had heard a good deal of talk through Maine about the burden of excessive railroad-freight charges, and got the impression that the railroads were taking too much toll of the State's products. When I visited the office of the State Railroad Commissioners I was informed that the first complaint of excessive charges that had been laid before the commission since it was established had then just been received. If the railroads of Maine are charging excessive freight rates the shippers have not seen fit to complain to the commission about it. The Maine Railroad Commission is supported by the railroads, not voluntarily, but by State decree, and most of its activity is spent in seeing to it that track and rolling stock are kept up to standard. The loss of life on Maine railroads is much lower than the average loss of life on the railroads of the country, as a result of this close paternal inspection.

Maine's Wonderful Apples and Potatoes

The sixty thousand farms in Maine are estimated to yield an annual average revenue of $500. gross, each, or a total of $30,000,000. The potato-fields of Aroostook County alone will this year earn for their owners close to $5,000,000 from that single crop and its by-products. Fourteen million bushels is the estimated shipment for the season, and the growers get an average price, at the railroad, of one dollar a barrel. The average cost of growing and delivering them at the railroad is sixty-five cents a barrel, leaving a fair margin.

In the potato industry, as in the apple industry of Maine, the growers have not yet availed themselves of the modern commercial device of coöperation for mutual benefit. At each of the many small stations on the Bangor & Aroostook Railroad in Aroostook County are from a dozen to fifty buyers for Boston and New York potato-jobbers. The middlemen take a large part of the price that the retailer has to pay for the potatoes in their ultimate markets. The dollar a barrel paid to the grower becomes a dollar a bushel in most retail markets, or close to three dollars a barrel. So with the apple-growers. Maine apples, as fine as any grown anywhere in this country, bring their growers an average price little if any above $1.25 a barrel, net. The grower pays twenty-five cents for a barrel and sells his fruit for $1.50 at the railroad. In the Boston and New York markets this price is doubled and not seldom tripled or quadrupled to the retail buyer. Half a million barrels of Maine apples annually find a market in Europe. The apple-growers of the States of Washington, Oregon, and Colorado, keener to take advantage of new commercial ideas, box their apples, which are decidedly inferior to Maine apples in every detail save looks, and get as much for a bushel of them as the Maine apple-grower gets for a barrel of his superior fruit. Here where boxwood is so plenty boxes to hold a barrel of apples could be made for the cost of a barrel. If the Maine apple-growers chose to manage their business as do their Western brothers they could easily double their revenue from this fruit, without increasing the retail prices in the city markets. It might be necessary for them to form associations, with selling-agencies in the larger cities, following the plan of the onion-growers of Texas, and other progressive agriculturists. When I suggested this plan to certain Maine apple-growers — mighty keen, shrewd individuals they were, too — each one grinned and said, "It may work in Texas, but it would n't work in Maine. Each member of the association would be afraid that his neighbor was getting a shade better treatment than himself."

Coming back to the topic of foreign immigration into Maine, it appears that until very recently almost the only foreigners in the State were French Canadians, who settled in the mill cities and supplied a large part of the labor in the cotton and woolen mills of the State. During the last two or three years many of these people have left the mills for more profitable employment elsewhere, and their places have been taken by Armenians, Italians, and Poles. There is now, as always, a large percentage of native Americans in the mills.

Large Recent Growth of Manufactures

The only available statistics concerning Maine manufacturing establishments are found in the bulletin of the United States Census Bureau for 1905. In that bulletin it appears that the number of establishments (not counting small concerns in which manufacturing was incidental to mercantile or other business or in which the value of the products for the year was less than $500) was 3,145, as compared with 2,878 in 1900. The capital invested in 1900 was $114,007,-715; in 1905, $143,707,750. The wage-earners in 1900 numbered 74,958, and the salaried officials, clerks, etc., 3,103, as against 74,958 and 3,772 in 1905. The total wages in 1905 were $32,691,759, a gain of nearly seven millions over 1900. The number of children under sixteen years employed in these establishments in 1900, according to the bulletin, was 2,175, as against only 1,471 in 1905. If these last figures were dependable, they would indicate an improving condition in the matter of the employment of child labor in Maine; but I find certain other statistics — this time compiled by an officer of the State of Maine — that give another color to this question.

Where Are the Missing Children?

In the Maine School Report for 1906 I find that whereas the number of children of school age in the city of Biddeford, one of the chief cotton-milling cities of Maine, is 6,023, the number registered at the spring term of public schools was 1,051. Where are the other 4,972 children of Biddeford? Are not fully half of them employed in the great cotton-mills? Did I err in believing that I saw hundreds of them, and scores of them less than twelve years of age, in the regiments of workers that entered the cotton-mills of Biddeford and Saco when the gates opened for them just after six o'clock on certain wintry mornings in late March? I fear not. I fear that my judgment of the situation was correct, and that, in violation of her laws, in violation of the rights of childhood, in violation of the State's best interests in its one most important crop,— her sons and daughters,— Maine is indeed selling her children into labor slavery to make dividends for non-resident capitalists.

Let us consider the case of the Pepperell Mills, the finest and most profitable in Maine. In these mills all the conditions are above the average. Through the executive genius of Mr. McArthur, the agent of these great mills, they have for twenty years produced for their owners — resident most of them in Massachusetts — annual dividends never less than twelve per cent, and sometimes as high as sixteen. Besides these regular dividends, the Pepperell Mills have produced in twenty years special or extra dividends amounting to 230 per cent. It seems fair to assume, a want of precise information, that the earnings of the Pepperell Mills for twenty years past have averaged nearly or quite twenty-five per cent per annum. During that period the average wages of the men employed in the mills have been little if any in excess of $8 weekly; of the women, close to $7. The children are cheaper. Wages in the Pepperell Mills have been increased ten per cent since 1902. During that period the mills have repaid to their owners the entire face value of their stock holdings, at least.

The State levies low taxes on capital, gives it rebates, as we have seen, and protects its interests at every point. Are not the children of Maine entitled to some protection? True, the law regulating child labor in factories has been so amended that the child applying for employment must bring a certificate of birth, legally establishing its right to the employment asked for. But since the State's factory inspection is so formal and inefficient it is only too easy to evade the law. I heard of many cases where children as young as ten years were employed in cotton-mills, working ten hours a day for a pittance with which to help eke out the meager earnings of their parents. As one shrewd and sympathetic observer put it:

"Boys and girls grow up to be young men and women in the mills. They fall in love, like other human beings, and marry. In due time the wife has to leave the mills to bear a child. Within a few weeks she is back in the mill, and her child is left in other hands to be reared. At six or seven years the child is on the streets selling papers, or doing something else to earn a few pennies. At from ten to fifteen years the child enters the mills, to grow up there as its parents did, to marry as they did, and to bring into the world more children to feed the machines. Not a cheerful picture, is it? But I am happy to say that conditions in this respect are improving of late. We in Maine have given too much thought to dividends and too little to the problems of the living wage and the rights of children. The new Commissioner of Labor, Mr. Lyons, of Vinal Haven, will pretty certainly make further improvements."

The New Commissioner of Labor

I talked with Mr. Lyons at Augusta — a tall, rugged, kindly man, a workingman, granite-cutter by trade for forty years. In his trade, he said, the eight-hour day and the minimum wage of $3 was firmly established. A strong union of resolute men had won these conditions in several hard contests. He meant to do what he could to lessen the crime of child labor. He did not call it a crime, but I could not doubt he so regarded it. The funds at the disposal of his department for this work were small,—very small,— but he believed the Governor, a kind, clean, high-grade man, would help him get what money might be needed to do the work right. He wanted to employ a woman to go through the factories, some one who would understand, better than a man could, the needs of the women and children workers in the mills. The job be-

fore him was so large he hardly knew where to begin and he was n't sure of his fitness for it, but he meant to do his best. And in the straight, direct look of his eyes and the warm, strong grip of his big, firm hand there was assurance that he meant exactly what he said. He was aware that whatever he might do would excite opposition from the interests that profit from illegal child labor, but he counted on the Governor's support to see him through.

Children as a "Money Crop"

Now, lest we suppose Biddeford to be an exceptional city in respect to the small proportion of children of school age actually in school, let us examine the figures for other Maine cities. The "mill cities" of Maine are Biddeford, Saco, Waterville, Augusta, and Lewiston. Let us see what the figures for these cities show. In Lewiston in 1906 there were 8,018 children of school age, of whom only 2,002, or less than one-fourth, actually attended the spring term. In Saco there were 1,742 children of school age, of whom 773 were in school. In Waterville there were 3,171 children of school age, of whom 1,150 attended the public schools. In Augusta, the State capital, out of 3,202 children of school age, only 1,280 were in school. Portland, the metropolis of the State, had 15,249 children of school age, of whom nearly one-half, or 7,438 were registered and 6,217 actually attended the spring term. In Auburn, across the river from Lewiston, there were 4,229 children of school age, and 1,712, considerably less than one-half, were in school. The number of different pupils registered at both spring and winter terms was 2,055. And so the story runs, through the long list of Maine's chief towns. Making all due allowances for children educated in parochial and private schools, the figures on school attendance point only too clearly to the fact that Maine, in practice if not in public proclamation, regards her young children as one of her best "money crops."

The Maine laws forbid the employment of children under twelve years of age in any manufacturing or mechanical establishment. The penalty, laid upon both employer and parent, is a fine of from $25 to $50. Girls under eighteen and boys under sixteen are not to be employed in manufacturing or mechanical establishments more than ten hours daily — with certain exceptions in favor of the employer that practically nullify this provision. The punishment for violation is the same as for the employment of children under twelve years of age. Mr. George E. Morrison, of Biddeford, State Inspector of factories, workshops, mines, and quarries, reports that he has found very many violations of the child-labor law. In one case he sent as many as sixty children out of one mill in a single week. But, he adds, all were hired on the strength of certificates falsely sworn to by parents or guardians, thus relieving the employer of legal responsibility and placing the legal penalty on the parents or guardians. Of all these, Mr. Morrison says, only one in a group of sixteen could read the certificates in English. They were French-Canadians, and were so poor that if the inspector had proceeded against them in court not one of the number could have paid the fine.

The average wages of men teachers in Maine are $38.99 per month, or $350.91 for nine months' working-time. The average weekly wage of women teachers in Maine is $7.48, or less than $300 for nine months' working-time.

The University a Live Factor

The State University of Maine is a thoroughly alive institution. Seven hundred young men and women are there at work. Less than twoscore of them aim at the A.B. degree. Most of them are studying in the several industrial departments. Engineering, agriculture, forestry, electricity, and the like practical pursuits appeal to the genius of young Maine. No other institution in the State returns equal dividends upon the money invested in it by the State, the common schools alone excepted. One department alone has earned and saved more money for Maine farmers than the whole cost of the university since its foundation.

This department — the Maine Agricultural Experiment Station — makes investigations upon the diseases of plants, injurious and beneficial insects, orcharding, the food and nutrition of man, poultry management, and the production of farm crops.

Since its establishment, in 1885, many results have been obtained which are of practical value to the farmers of Maine. Perhaps the two most striking illustrations have to do with the potato crop and the poultry industry. Prior to 1897 the potato-growing section of the State suffered greatly from potato rot. That year the experiment station began demonstration experiments which proved conclusively that the fungous disease which caused this rot and loss could be kept in check by the use of Bordeaux mixture, which is made from quicklime and copper sulphate. Spraying with these materials has rapidly developed, so that a single county uses at present about four hundred tons of copper sulphate on potato-vines annually. This has increased the yield about fifty per cent, and has changed an uncertain crop to a comparatively sure one. It is estimated by people not connected with the station that this treatment of potato-vines has increased the value of the crop by a million dollars a year.

Eight years ago the experiment station began to put the following question to poultry-growers: Is it possible by breeding from selected high layers to increase the egg-production? This has been answered in the affirmative by the several hundred hens that are carried by the station. Due to this breeding, there has been a steady increase from one hundred and twenty, eight years ago, until in 1906 the seven hundred pullets averaged one hundred and fifty eggs each in their first laying-year. While this benefit has been extended somewhat to the State by the selling of stock, it shows how great an increase at comparatively small cost can be had in this important industry.

In addition to work of investigation, certain police duties are entrusted to the director of the experiment station. These inspections of fertilizers, feeding-stuffs, agricultural seeds and food have been productive of much good. The longer inspections have been in force the more thorough the protection. Fertilizer inspection, which has been a feature of the work since 1885, has brought about the fact that there is not a pound of fraudulent fertilizer sold in the State. The law regulating the sale of concentrated commercial feeding-stuffs has been in force about ten years, to the marked improvement of the quality of the feeds. The inspection of agricultural seeds and food is recent, but there is every reason to believe that it will bring about the desired ends.

What's the matter with Maine? The niggardly treatment of the State's public schools is one thing; the land-grabbing, and tariff-wall building of past generations of public administrators are others. The tax-dodging by railroad and other corporations and owners of great tracts of wild lands, both past and present, adds to the list.

This, however, is from the view-point of the native. From that of the summer visitor, be he hunter, fisher, nature-student, or merely lucky idler in sun and shade, there is absolutely nothing the matter with Maine. It will be soon too hot to talk politics, reform, or any other serious subject. Meanwhile, Maine will welcome to her bays and lakes, her forests, streams, and mountains, a happy army of three hundred thousand visitors from other States, and will send them home in the fall renewed in health and strength and determined to come again if they can find the time and raise the money. Ask these people what's the matter with Maine and they will respond in one ringing chorus, "Maine's all right."

"HUNDRED-HARBORED MAINE"

A discussion of Maine's natural resources, industries, agriculture and people in celebration of her
Centennial.

Review of Reviews, July, 1920.

"HUNDRED-HARBORED MAINE"

THE YOUNGEST OF THE NEW ENGLAND STATES IN HER CENTENNIAL YEAR

BY WILLIAM I. COLE

PORTLAND HEAD LIGHT

WHOEVER first applied to Maine the Hom-eric-sounding phrase "the hundred - har-bored" character-ized, picturesquely and aptly, this the twenty - third State of the Union. The coast of Maine, al-though less than 200 miles long, measured in a straight line, presents through its sinu-osities a sea frontage of nearly 3000 miles. This fringe-like edge, moreover, is tasseled with bold promontories and rocky islands, thus affording many a fiord-like harbor, to which the islands give added protection. In-deed, between Portland and Eastport it con-tains a far greater number of deep and well-sheltered harbors than any other stretch of coast of equal length along the Atlantic sea-board.

A Region of Forests, Lakes, and Rivers

An even greater natural asset of Maine than its harbors are its vast forests of spruce, hemlock, balsam-fir, maple, oak, and other useful trees, huge sections of which are still practically untouched. Its primeval forests of pine, which gave to Maine the name of the Pine Tree State have unfortunately al-most wholly disappeared, although partially replaced by a second growth. To-day the most abundantly growing and characteristic tree of the State is the spruce rather than the pine.

In 1846, Thoreau described the scene from the summit of Mt. Katahdin, the highest point of land in the State. "No clearing, no house," he says. "Countless lakes—Moosehead in the southwest, forty miles long by ten wide, like a gleaming silver plat-ter at the end of the table; Chesuncook, eighteen long by three wide, without an island; Millinocket, on the south, with its hundred islands; and a hundred others with-out a name; and mountains, also, whose names, for the most part, are known only to the Indians. The forest looked like a firm grass sward, and the effect of these lakes in its midst has been well compared to that of a mirror broken into a thousand frag-ments, and wildly scattered over the grass, reflecting the full blaze of the sun." The hermit of Walden Pond, should he return to the same spot to-day would find the scene little changed.

Rivaling in importance its forests and harbors are the rivers of Maine. Aside from the excellent inland waterways that some of these afford, particularly the Penobscot and the Kennebec, their falls and rapids, if prop-erly harnessed, would, so it has been esti-mated, do the work of 2,000,000 horses. No less important are the lakes, 1600 in number, which not only serve as reservoirs for the rivers and almost innumerable streams, which cover the State as with a piece of wide-flung lace, but contribute not a little toward making Maine what it is and long has been, a place sought more and more by nature-lovers and sportsmen. The area of the State, I might add, is only a little less than that of all the rest of New England.

Aside from its extensive quarries of granite, slate, limestone, and feldspar, Maine is not, however, especially rich in mineral resources. But one other exception should be noted—its springs of mineral waters, the repute of which is world-wide.

The Search for Norumbega

Visions of the mythical Norumbega, "with its columns of crystal and silver," lured not a few of the early discoverers to this general region, which, later, was designated in the charter of Charles I as the "Province or Countie of Mayne," because regarded as part of "the Mayne land of New England." Before the middle of the sixteenth century one and another of these explorers had sailed up the Penobscot River in search of this splendid city where, if Hakluyt in his "Principall Navigations" is to be believed, the inhabitants wore heavy ornaments of gold, richest furs were plentiful, and rubies six inches long were a common sight. Norumbega was never found on the Penobscot or anywhere else, for it was a city of the imagination; but to the search for it was due, in a measure at least, the fact that in Maine were the historical beginnings of New England.

Maine Colonized Before the Pilgrims Landed

Thirteen years before the landing of the Pilgrims at Plymouth, a company of 120 colonists went ashore at a place near the mouth of the Kennebec and proceeded to build for themselves some fifty cabins, with storehouses, chapel and a fort. The undertaking was shortlived, to be sure, but from that time on until the establishment of the first permanent settlement within its boundaries, at Pemaquid, in 1625, Maine was not wholly without settlers—the French Jesuits on Mt. Desert, numerous fishermen associated with them on the same island, and other fishermen on the Island of Monhegan. "Welcome Englishmen," Samoset's greeting in the English tongue which so startled the newly-arrived Pilgrims at Plymouth, can be explained only by the fact that this "Lord of Pemaquid" had had at home intercourse with Englishmen. At Monhegan, in 1622, Governor Winslow, so he tells us, found food for the suffering Pilgrims. Thus Maine was peopled, if not settled, before Massachusetts or any other part of New England, a fact for which the search for splendid but elusive Norumbega was in some measure responsible.

Maine's Independent Spirit

That Maine should, sooner, or later, be set off from Massachusetts, to which without as much as a "by your leave" it had been annexed in 1691, was inevitable. It was not an offshoot or a colony of Massachusetts, as the story of its historical beginnings shows. Then, too, the Maine people early gave evidence of a marked spirit of self-reliance and a willingness and capacity to take care of themselves. Nowhere were these traits more conspicuously shown than in the so-called first naval battle of the Revolution, which was fought in Machias Bay, an indentation of the extreme eastern coast of the State.

When the British gunboat, the *Margaretta*, convoying certain small sloops in search of lumber to be used by the British troops in Boston, sailed into this bay, the men of the vicinity, taking counsel only with themselves, seized such weapons as were at hand, including scythes and pitchforks, and made a spirited attack upon the enemy. All the officers and members of the crew of the gunboat were killed or captured and the vessel itself was sunk. This unique victory by the men of Machias, acting on their own initiative, is commemorated to-day in the names borne by two of our naval vessels, the gunboat *Machias* and the torpedo-boat *O'Brien* —Jeremiah O'Brien having been the name of the leader in the attack.

There were also other reasons, geographical, political, social, and economic, why the separation of Maine from Massachusetts was merely a question of time. Maine was, for instance, anti-Federalist, or Democratic, and as such felt, naturally, little sympathy with Federalist Massachusetts. Perhaps, also, Maine saw in its severance from its guardian State an easy escape from the burdensome debt incurred by Massachusetts during the two wars with Great Britain. Maine people have always been thrifty-minded.

Hardly was the Revolution at an end, when Maine began to take steps toward detaching itself from Massachusetts. There is little doubt, however, that it would have been much longer than it was in achieving this purpose had not the controversy arisen over the admission of Missouri into the Union. That struggle, it will be recalled, brought about the necessity of taking one more northern State into the Union to preserve the balance of power. Here, then, was an unexpected opportunity of which, as we may feel assured, Maine was not slow to take the fullest advantage; for Maine people have always been amply endowed with shrewdness. Exactly one hundred years ago its separation from Massachusetts was finally effected and Maine, erected into a State, was received into the Union. Inevitable as it was, forty years of serious although intermittent effort were required to bring this result about; and then, when it was accomplished, it was merely a part of the Missouri Compromise! Such are often the ways of Fate!

If I were asked what is the greatest product of Maine, I would answer without hesitation, "Its eminent sons and daughters." These are, of course, a product whose importance cannot be stated in dollars and cents but only in terms of spiritual value. Let anyone follow back to their native lairs the statesmen, writers, inventors, merchants, philanthropists, educators, military leaders, theologians, journalists, artists, jurists, actors, and "captains of industry," past and present, whose names occurred to him the most readily, and he will be surprised to find how many of them take him to Maine.

Hannibal Hamlin, John D. Long, Thomas B. Reed, Roswell D. Hitchcock, Samuel Harris and his nephew George Harris, Egbert C. Smythe and his brother Newman Smythe, Henry W. Longfellow, George Hillard, John S. C. Abbott, N. P. Willis, Elijah Kellogg, Harriet Prescott Spofford, Annie Louise Cary, Lillian Norton, known on the stage as Lillian Nordica; Sarah Orne Jewett, Kate Douglas Wiggin, Frederic P. Vinton, Lillian M. N. Stevens, Sol Smith Russell, Marcella Crafts, Maxine Elliott and her sister, Gertrude Elliott; Arlo Bates, Holman Day, Eben D. Jordan, Jacob Sleeper, Hiram Maxim, Dorothea L. Dix, Charles F. Thwing, "Artemus Ward," Oliver O. Howard — these are only a few of the Maine men and women, jotted down almost at random, who have achieved far more than ordinary distinction in some line of human thought and endeavor. To the same, goodly company belong Melville W. Fuller, for twenty-two years Chief Justice of the United States; Edward P. Mitchell, editor of the New York Sun; John Knowles Paine, musical composer; James R. Day, university chancellor; Frank A. Munsey, publisher; Donald B. MacMillan, arctic explorer; Samuel V. Cole, college president and poet; H. W. Savage and Edward F. Albee, theatrical managers, and many another. The rivers of genius have watered Maine no less abundantly than its lace-work of natural rivers and streams.

These and the host of others who belong in the same category, represent an output of brains and brawn, of moral courage and physical daring, high moral ideals, patriotic endeavor, and noble aspiration, which, could it be rendered in terms of dollars and cents, would far exceed in value Maine's output in granite and lumber, of ice and potatoes, great as that is. Maine is first of all a producer of men and women.

The Mecca of Vacation-Seekers

Much might be said of Maine as a rest resort and the paradise of the hunter and fisherman. Here, in ever increasing numbers, the "tired business man," that object of special solicitude on the part of the theatrical manager, comes with his family; and in hotel, cottage, or camp, on the seacoast or by river or lake, or in the "silent places" of the great woods, finds healthful change and relief. While the wicked may not cease altogether from troubling, the weary man can be, relatively at least, at rest. For the sportsmen, Maine is superabounding in allurements. There are wild geese, woodcock quail, plover, partridge, and almost every kind of duck found in North America in the heavens above—at greater or less elevations; moose, deer, bear, and rabbits, on the earth beneath; and trout, bass, togue and salmon in the waters under the earth. Not far from 2800 licenses for hunting have been issued to non-residents in a single year, while the multitude coming into the State annually to try "fisherman's luck," no man can number. It is estimated that fully a half-million of people visit Maine every year for purposes of recreation or sport—a total that is two-thirds that of the State's entire population.

But Maine welcomes all comers, its returning sons and daughters and the stranger alike, and gives them access to all of its best. Its latch-string is always out; and at this time when it is celebrating the completion of one hundred years of Statehood, those who have ever enjoyed its hospitality will join with its absentee sons and daughters, its children at home, and all its friends everywhere, in wishing it health and prosperity for centuries to come.

Hail, "hundred-harbored Maine"!

MAINE COAST PHILOSOPHY

The following describes the individuals who live along the coast, their attitudes and the means by which they earn their livelihoods by fishing.

Atlantic Monthly, July, 1923

MAINE COAST PHILOSOPHY

BY RAY MORRIS

I

LET us take our location and background well east, where the fog is always ready to drift in from the sea, against the spruce trees that rise in ragged outline above the granite shore. The day has five requirements to be met and dealt with, each with its own ceremonial: food, water, wood, ice, and garbage! These are very ancient necessities, but the city, by intensive organization, has taken away from many of us the curious pleasure of dealing with them directly. The city makes us forget what our grandfathers knew; how much more diverting it can be to keep the machinery of life running than it is to provide conscious amusement for one's self.

The camp usually starts the day with the water problem, which is wholly in the hands of a minor but capable gasolene engine; an engine of infinite personality, ready to perform its whole duty with a merry heart if, and only if, it is dealt with in a spirit of sympathy and understanding. There are, I believe, mechanical souls, born that way, to whom the care of a temperamental engine presents neither problem nor amusement; of them I speak not. This record is the record of the thoroughly non-mechanical city man, who has these things done for him at home, either by John, or by somebody who is telephoned to in the village.

But the camp has neither John, nor telephone: if we ourselves cannot make the engine run, the penalty is immedi-ate, and the camp must go without water, at least in quantity. This bald statement of fact is not intended to be a threat, however; we can make the engine run, most of the time, and we take the special pleasure in dry cells, igniters, and gaskets that comes with the partial attainment of any unfamiliar handicraft. When the engine is running sweetly, with the proper number of explosions to the minute, we wipe our hands on our khaki trousers, with a profound sense of satisfaction and accomplishment. The morning pipe tastes best then, and there is nothing but friendly comradeship in the passing comment of the gulls watching over the pump-house cove.

The charm of getting in the ice is more obscure; it arises, I think, from determined and successful dealing with a rather unscrupulous adversary; cold, wet, slippery, and intensely heavy by nature, with no thought of meeting you halfway. What the ice would best like to do is to remain frozen in the floor of the house in the woods, where it has been spending the summer; it would also like immensely to wet you thoroughly with enormously cold water, and then slip off on your foot. But you circumvent it and defeat it at every turn. Your first weapon is a very mighty one — the crowbar. Then, the piece of ice being fairly ejected, torn loose from its stronghold by superior intelligence, aided by the mechanical principle of the lever, you turn its own natural attributes against it. It wants to slip; it shall slip, therefore, into the wheelbarrow. It is inordinately heavy, but the camp is down hill from the ice-house, so we need merely restrain it in its natural instinct to go down hill.

To get it into the ice-box requires a lift, and various fittings and chippings. We used to lift the ice against our bosom, strainingly, wetly, and coldly; we did not know any better, because we were raised in the city. Now, however, we use ice-tackle, with the mechanical aid of two double blocks, and we play again on an unsuspected weakness in ice character. Ice can never resist the driven sharp point, that is, the ice-tongs; but, the point once in, it applies all its massive, silly stubbornness against any tearing-out process which would so easily release it. And so the 'piece' is tonged and swung up on the block tackle, all without effort or struggle. We have learned what the country all around us always knew; we have relearned what our grandfathers knew. Not only have we got the ice in, but we have not exerted ourselves!

The infinite range and variety of things which the Maine native can cause to happen without exerting himself, is worthy a separate study. Take, for example, the setting of my mooring: a native boulder weighing some fifteen hundred pounds, which was induced to leave its chosen resting-place at the head of the cove, and moved a quarter of a mile into position. And nobody exerted himself!

The manner of it was this. On a rising tide, a stout dory was floated over the boulder, and chains, with a device to trip them, were passed under the boulder and around the comfortable waist of the dory. It was time, then, for the attendants to smoke their pipes and watch the tide rise. Two hours later, the dory, a little flushed, but triumphant, floated away with the

boulder under it. In the proper part of the cove the chain was tripped and the mooring set — and nobody had exerted himself; nobody, that is, except the tide and the dory.

But we are gossiping when we ought to be at work. At this time of day, it would be better if we were to go for a row with the garbage, intending, quite frankly, to come back alone! Should this seem too definite a yielding to poor company, let us hasten to assure you that this is one of our best overtures to nature, always ready to provide amusement in these latitudes. The point of the adventure being, not the garbage, but the sea gulls, who go so far out of their way to show what basely material souls may be hidden beneath a snowy exterior.

There is only one gull about when we issue the invitation to the banquet, and that one is far overhead, aloof, and rather coldly majestic. He comes down immediately, however; finds, to his regret, that he is not as courageous in our presence as he supposed he would be; and circles away again, rather anxiously. Then there is a rush of wings as two other gulls arrive, at great speed, out of nowhere, bank against the breeze, and alight.

Our first guest rather feared that this would happen. He returns, nervously; finds a great sense of security in the society of others; and joins the party with eager haste and a certain laying aside of dignity.

Somebody has to squawk, now. I am sure it is unintentional, or at least not intended to arouse the neighbors, because there is nothing ostensibly co-operative in sea-gull nature. But somebody squawks.

And now the Folly Island squad arrives, skimming very close to the water. A gull does this when he is in a special hurry; optical illusion, perhaps, because the sense of progress, twelve inches above the water, must be tremendous.[1]

Now forty gulls have accepted our invitation; now seventy; now a hundred, and it is not yet five minutes since the table, so to speak, was set. Looking at this matter purely from the gulls' standpoint, and disregarding entirely any question of personal taste in viands, we cannot get away from the feeling that this mad competition, this dreadful urgency to arrive ahead of one's neighbor, and the consequent necessity of bolting one's food, mars an existence that might otherwise be almost idyllic. The gull has a singularly beautiful person; he enjoys admirable health and vigor, lives to an advanced age, and carries himself on his solitary watches with the pride and dignity of the elder Cato. How sad, therefore, that his true life, lying so near the surface, should be intensely acrimonious, bitter, and greedy.

Taste, we know, is not debatable; there are certain refinements which seem important to us and do not seem important to the gull, and that is all there is to it. But to feel obliged to bolt whole a thorny sea-perch a foot long, afterward shaking the tail convulsively, to register success and satisfaction — this does not go with the demeanor and bearing of a Cato; it makes life less worth while, somehow. A hundred gulls, living together on a reef in a state of suspended hostility, seem all to keep fit and to get plenty to eat between these mad and rather unproductive rushes after the boat that is cleaning fish, or the other sudden and unexpected banquets that get provided from time to time. It may be, then,

[1] We have discussed this point with Mr. Orville Wright who says the gull is right and we are wrong. By flying close to the water, the gull brings about a sort of air-compression beneath his wings, and increases his pace. — THE AUTHOR.

that we are dealing merely with the pleasure of the chase, which often assumes strange forms. But if it is socially and athletically important to arrive instantly at every fish-cleaning, every garbage party, the nervous strain must indeed be great, and ever present. No wonder that dispositions get tense and crabbed and that the vocabulary of the sport is rude and hasty.

II

In discussing the camp's food-supply, let us touch lightly on the semiweekly trip to town in the car, and the effort, on the return trip, to separate and keep separate the children, the kerosene, the leg of lamb, the sugar, and the bread. We buy meats and groceries, but the charm of the general store, down by the fish-wharf, with its tempting cod-lines, hooks, and sinkers, marine hardware, and, of course, gasolene, dry cells, and 'Fig Newtons,' is less than the special joys attendant upon the direct pursuit of fish and berries. These the camp provides for itself, with much organization and ritual.

Nobody wants to eat a sea-perch, for example, although he abounds in our waterways. But the cod; his red cousin the rock cod; the pollock, the haddock, and the flounder, — disgraceful in his personal tastes but objectively delicious, — all these are eagerly sought, and each is a highly specialized character, with habits and customs that may be odd, but must be respected.

Consider this matter of catching a big cod. The supper-table size is rather plentiful; but the forty-pounders require organization — something akin really to folk-lore. The local marine characters, and their fathers and grandfathers before them, take and have taken the same 'ranges' to get the big fellows. You get the spindle in line with Schoodic Point; then you bisect with a line from the church-steeple to the outer corner of the Ducks. At the intersection is a famous feeding ground — or a sanitarium, perhaps — for stout, elderly cod. To induce them on board the launch is no matter of dainty casts, light rods, and carefully selected flies. The elderly cod are seventy-five feet or so below the surface, and have made all their arrangements to stay there. Two enormous hooks, clam-baited and attached to a sort of clothes-line, weighted down with a couple of pounds of lead, constitute an almost undeclinable invitation, however.

The big cod takes your bait in a leisurely way; he does not hurry, nor does he want to be hurried, and landing him is something like frisking a trunk out of the hold of a steamer. But the thrill is there! Your passenger, as he approaches the surface of the water, is enormous, — unbelievably enormous; and your personal satisfaction goes back, no doubt, to old barbarous beginnings. This thing is huge; it did not want to be caught, and you have caught it and intend to eat it — or a pound or two of it! Do not inquire whether the point of view is so particularly different from that of the sea gull triumphantly bolting a perch two sizes too big for the obvious limitations of comfort and digestion. Perhaps the strong sea air makes us alike barbaric; we do not know, nor do we care; we have caught a big cod, and would very likely swallow it whole, if our mouths were not so absurdly small.

For a touch of sporting gayety, the plunging, rearing, dashing kind of fish, either the pollock or the haddock, will satisfy. The pollock is a silvery, lavender-shaded fish, built along speed lines. The haddock is much the same shape, but has decorated himself in a grotesque, court-beauty manner: a 'stream line' on each side, and one great foolish spot of purple, quite unconnected with the general design, but very fetching, nevertheless. Either of these fast-moving gentlemen knows how to impersonate a salmon; and if you get two at once, as you often do,— one on each hook, and splitting tacks on the way up, — you have no doubt that you have caught something. The cod rests ponderously on or near the bottom; the pollock and the haddock are always going somewhere, or coming from somewhere, in a great hurry, and half-way to the surface.

I am a little ashamed to talk about flounder-fishing, but let us be frank with each other. The way to catch flounder, breakfast size, is to have a flounder garden to catch them out of; the way to plant a flounder garden is always to clean your fish off the float. But let us not examine this subject further. You do not wonder what the flounder finds to eat one half as dainty as he is himself; you know what he finds to eat, because you put it there for him. Although we have had more personal experience with the care and feeding of flounders than with the care and feeding of pigs, our country background prompts the impression that we admire bacon in spite of, rather than because of, the varied and somewhat hasty diet of the pig.

III

There is so much to Maine coast deep-sea fishing, besides the culinary and sporting aspects, however, that we must not dwell too long on these. The foundation of it all is the launch; and the foundation of launch navigation is dry cells and gasolene, those prime staples of marine life east of Rockland. We speak not of mahogany speedabouts: we mean the native launch — one cylinder, make-and-break; and you mix your lubricating oil with your gasolene in the tank forward. We do not operate with a captain; why should we delegate to another the thrilling satisfaction of training that one-cylinder engine to heel; of making it go when you want to, and of diagnosing and remedying its absurd complaints? Enslaved, illogical, elate, we greet the embarrassed marine gods. Much of navigating, much of marine engineering, we do wrong; but we have left untouched all the principal reefs, and, as we write, we are safely at home, after dealing with fog, smoky southwesters, and carbon on the igniter. *Gaudeamus, igitur, juvenes dum sumus!*

The best time of day on the Maine coast, is early in the morning. It is also by far the most fashionable time of day to begin launch operations. Lie at anchor in Burnt Coat Harbor, and note the time of day when the line fishermen get under way for their day's work. About dawn the *put-put-putter* out of the harbor begins. Some of the boats syncopate, while cold in the morning. Others are loud, clear, and amazingly punctual in their explosions. One we named the Peter Piper, because it dealt so accurately with the line about the peck of pickled peppers.

Dawn is too early for us, however; but about seven o'clock the sea air is wonderfully fragrant; the early morning mists are rising, and the gray, unpainted wharf, with the gray, unpainted sheds on it and around it, and the quick, stirring boat-life all about, is a charming thing. In common with the camp dog, we like the smell of the Maine coast as well as anything else about it, and it is at its very best in these early hours.

Nor is the enjoyment lessened by the thrilling fact that we may have a little fog navigating to do. Our compass is of the best; but a launch is a very receptacle of iron, in all shapes and forms, from the engine to the anchor, and

launch compasses are given to listening to strange voices of attraction. Do not suppose, therefore, that you can parallel-rule your course on the chart and steer it by compass; you will get somewhere, no doubt, but your landfalls will be a bit sketchy. Open-and-shut, or glimpse, navigating in the fog, is easy, safe, and thrilling, however. You know pretty well the direction from your own harbor to Moose Island, and so you set for Moose, observing what course the compass pleases to call it with the anchor where it is. That course you hold, through the fog, and fetch Moose Island squarely. Then you get an approximate bearing; edge in to the shore, and eventually pick up Goose Cove Rock, identifying it readily by its scaffolding for tarring weir-nets. And so on, down the coast, proceeding from the known to the unknown, and anchoring in cases of extreme doubt. If you have judged your day shrewdly, the sun has burned the fog off before you get to the fishing-ground; meanwhile, the only traffic to look out for are the lobstermen, examining their traps and picking them up out of the murk, one after the other, with an unerring, compassless certainty which suggests the carrier pigeon.

A lobster, gridiron-cooked on a rocky island over a driftwood fire, is one of the very good things of this coast; but the lobsterman does other things, too, for your pleasure. During the fall and winter he digs and 'shucks' enormous quantities of clams beside his little workshop on a sheltered, diminutive cove. The piles of shells furnish a marvelous fertilizer, and wild raspberries, of great size and lusciousness, grow in profusion beside the shells. The pursuit of berries sounds a bit maiden-auntly for a camping party; but set out some early morning in the launch, with the lobster workshop coves and the shells as your objective, and you will spend your time with much satisfaction.

Among the daily camp responsibilities, we have not spoken, nor do we intend to speak, of 'wooding,' except to observe that it is one of the best of sports for a week-end, and easily the worst for a month. Driftwood plays a fascinating part, while it lasts; but the chopping and bucksawing of trees, afterward splitting the billets to stove size, is one of those clinging, obdurate jobs, which eventually embitters the soul.

There is another reason, too, for buying wood. This country of the east Maine coast abounds in shy, friendly characters, who make gently helpful suggestions, and are most efficient in meeting your wants, if you will let them. What else they find to live on is a study in itself. One charming neighbor of ours 'lobsters' for a living. He is in the sixties, wears spectacles, smokes a pipe, and presents an altogether serene picture of contentment and human satisfaction. Unmarried, he has a bit of a farm, but it is doubtful if he sells any produce from it. He rises at four, fishes for sculpin, — that amazingly thorny, unsatisfactory fish, so beloved by the lobster, — baits his traps, resets them, and is back in the cove again by nine, ready for lunch, I believe it is. He tells us he often takes in a hundred dollars from his lobstering in a good year. Other cash resources are not in evidence; I do not believe they amount to much.

A little farming; some work on the roads; a certain amount of 'wooding' in the winter; odd carpentering jobs, and work on and around the boats and the weirs — this is what our east coast mostly lives by. Weir-fishing — the construction and operation of these great marine mouse-traps, stretching out from the local headlands to intercept the shoals of herring that subse-

quently become dignified into sardines —is, in spots, a considerable industry, and the factories at Bass Harbor and Southwest Harbor are kept busy. But I suppose no business is more utterly speculative. The Maine coast does not gamble in oil-stocks, but it does gamble in weirs; and many a local little fortune of a thousand dollars or so, plus what the weir-builder can borrow, goes the way of the white alley. When 'sardines' take a streak of running into your weir, you may take in forty, or sixty, or a hundred dollars a day. The sardine boat from the factory *put-puts* merrily into your cove; the nets from the storage part of the weir pour a shining flood of herring into the dories, and the fishermen, in their hip-boots, wade waist-deep in herring, as they shovel them into the sardine boat, receiving spot cash on the basis of the estimated capacity of the dory. But weirs, at present prices for twine and labor, cost perhaps two thousand dollars to make; the nets must be cared for, repaired, and retarred at the curious little tarring stations; stakes must be set by floating pile-driver—and then the fish go away, as quickly and silently as they came; or else, in their abundance, the bottom falls out of the market; the factories are overstocked, and the sardine boat no longer calls. Weir-building goes in waves: in the latter part of the war it was extremely active and temporarily profitable; but now most of the nets are up, on the section of the coast by the camp, and there remain only the stakes, highly dangerous to launch navigation at high tide — and the unpaid debts for twine and labor.

At the height of the speculation, a thoroughly interesting thing to do was to row out to the weir at sunrise and see the fishermen appraising their catch. Each new day brought its fascinating possibilities of sudden profit; and a gallery of directly interested sea gulls added a touch of color and of subdued but eager comment.

But the day's work at the camp is done, though we have been long enough about it. There now remains the peculiar and special pleasure of a game of chess, sweetened by tobacco-smoke and the sense of a considerable amount of physical labor punctiliously performed, and followed by a very brief swim in what is probably the coldest unfrozen water in the world. Around sunset we shall have visitors: a party of loons may choose this evening for a perfectly absurd and screamingly noisy 'jazz' party in the cove, dashing about half out of the water, and shouting with laughter. Later on, the heron will probably come by, in the dusk, flying heavily, and remarking 'crawk' loudly and critically from time to time. The contrast between the impatient, middle-aged dissatisfaction of the heron and the adolescent, flapper gayety of the loon is ridiculous. We wonder, lightly, if the heron was never young, and if the congenial party of loon never grow old, or, if so, how it affects their conduct of life. We think, also, of the sea gull that swallowed whole the perch with all the bones, scales, and so forth, appurtenant thereto, and wonder if it is still perfectly comfortable and self-composed. On the whole, we believe so, though we do not know why.

Finally, we get around to the philosophy of living in perfect contentment on a hundred dollars, cash, per year. Are we really any better off than the lobsterman, and is he really happier than the sea gull, or the irrepressible loon? We do not know, but we do not propose to worry about it, because it is bedtime.

BASIC FACTS

Capital: Augusta.
Largest City: Portland.
Nicknames: Pine Tree State; Old Dirigo.
Song: "State of Maine Song."
Abbreviation: ME.

23rd State to enter Union, March 15, 1820.
Area: 33,215 sq. mi.
Population (1970 Census): 997,000.

State Tree: Western White Pine.

State Bird: Chickadee.

State Flower: White Pine Cone & Tassel.

State Bird : Chickadee

State Flower : White Pine Cone & Tassel

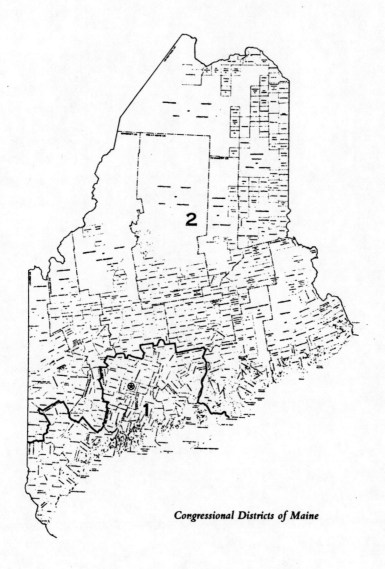

Congressional Districts of Maine

SELECTED BIBLIOGRAPHY

Abbott, John Stewart Cabot and E. H. Elwell. The History of Maine. Portland: Brown, Thurston Co., 1892.

Coe, Harriet Badger, ed. Maine, Resources, Attractions and Its People; A History. 4 vols. New York: The Lewis Historical Publishing Co., Inc., 1928

Coffin, Robert Peter Tristram. Kennebec, Cradle of Americans. New York and Toronto: Farrar & Rinehart, Inc., 1937.

Elkins, L. Whitney. The Story of Maine. Bangor, Me.: The Hillsborough Co., 1924.

Hatch, Louis Clinton, ed. in chief. Maine: A History. 5 vols. New York: The American Historical Co., 1919.

Jewett, Fred Eugene. A Financial History of Maine. New York: Columbia University Press, 1937.

Kallenbach, Joseph E. and Jessamine S. Kallenbach. American State Governors, 1776-1976. 3 vols. Dobbs Ferry, N. Y.: Oceana Publications, Inc., 1977-

Roberts, Kenneth Lewis. Trending Into Maine. Boston: Little, Brown and Co., 1938.

Rowe, William Hutchinson. The Maritime History of Maine. New York: W. W. Norton, 1948.

Sawtelle, William Otis. Historic Trails and Waterways of Maine. Augusta, Me.: Maine Development Commission, 1932.

Smith, Marion Jacques. A History of Maine from Wilderness to Statehood. Portland: Falmouth Publishing House, 1949.

Smith, Zachariah Frederick. The History of Kentucky. Louisville: Courier-Journal Job Printing Co., 1886.

Starkey, Glenn Wendell. Maine, Its History, Resources, and Government. 3rd ed. New York: Silver Burdett Co., 1938.

Sylvester, Herbert Milton. Maine Pioneer Settlements. 5 vols. Boston: W. B. Clarke Co., 1909.

Verrill, Alpheus Hyatt. Romantic and Historic Maine. New York: Dodd Mead & Co., 1933.

NAME INDEX